# 10
# MINUTE GUIDE TO

# INTRANETS

by MBR Consulting, Inc.

*A Division of Macmillan Computer Publishing*
*201 West 103rd St., Indianapolis, Indiana 46290 USA*

# ®1995 Que Corporation

International Standard Book Number: 0-7897-0855-8
Library of Congress Catalog Card Number: 96-68577

98 97 96   8 7 6 5 4 3 2 1

Interpretation of the printing code: the rightmost number of the first series of numbers is the year of the book's printing; the rightmost number of the second series of numbers is the number of the book's printing. For example, a printing code of 95-1 shows that the first printing of the book occurred in 1995.

Screen reproductions in this book were created by means of the program Collage Plus from Inner Media, Inc., Hollis, NH.

*Printed in the United States of America*

**Publisher:** Roland Elgey

**Vice-President and Publisher:** Marie Butler-Knight

**Editorial Services Director:** Elizabeth Keaffaber

**Publishing Manager:** Lynn Zingraff

**Managing Editor:** Michael Cunningham

**Development Editor:** Melanie Palaisa

**Production Editors:** Phil Kitchel, Katie Purdum

**Technical Editor:** Discovery Computing, Inc.

**Cover Designer:** Kim Scott

**Designer:** Barbara Kordesh

**Indexers:** Ginny Bess, Craig Small

**Production Team:** Stephen Adams, Jason Carr, Joan Evan, DiMonique Ford, Jessica Ford, Trey Frank, Jason Hand, Daryl Kessler, Michelle Lee, Casey Price, Kaylene Riemen, Laura Robbins, Bobbi Satterfield, Jeff Yesh

# CONTENTS

# INTRODUCTION

Imagine working in a company where, with the simple point and click of your PC mouse, you could:

- Receive training on personal or professional development topics, or on your company's new products or services.

- Access your company's up-to-date human resource information such as job openings or employee manuals.

- Communicate efficiently with coworkers regardless of their physical location.

- Retrieve information from diverse corporate databases.

- Stay current on corporate news and events.

- Move back and forth among all of these types of information effortlessly with the same software.

Futuristic? Wish list? Blue sky? Dream on? Not really!

These and other capabilities are currently becoming a reality in many corporations today through the use of *intranets*.

Business information is changing so rapidly that traditional methods of producing and disseminating printed materials don't work. Critical material is often out-of-date before it reaches the people who need it. In today's competitive business arena, timely access to accurate information is essential for corporate competitiveness and personal job satisfaction and success. The solution provided by intranets uses technology that can:

- Provide information on demand.

- Guarantee access to current, accurate, and consistent data.

- Allow information to be controlled by the people who prepare it.

- Operate on many different hardware platforms without conversion.

...and do it all cost-effectively.

Intranets are here *now*, and their application and use is exploding. Chances are your company is implementing one today or is about to in the near future. Pick up any newspaper or magazine and you are almost certain to find one or more articles discussing some new or expanded business use of the technology.

Experts say that understanding and being able to use corporate intranets is a necessary and essential job skill for information workers of all types.

# WELCOME TO THE 10 MINUTE GUIDE TO INTRANETS

You use a computer at work. You've been using Windows 95, and you regularly access your company's network. Most of you have heard of the Internet, and some of you may have even ventured onto it. Now your company's talking *intra*-net. Thinking that one "Net" is plenty, you're not quite sure what to make of this new addition to the Information Superhighway.

It's natural to assume that any computer system with the power and flexibility of intranets might be hard to learn. Nothing could be further from the truth. The consistency and simplicity of using intranet technology is the key element of its widespread growth and acceptability. The *10 Minute Guide to Intranets* will explain everything you need to know to be confident using your organization's current or future intranet. The lessons are brief, straightforward, and written in language that is easy to understand.

This book is intended for anyone interested in learning:

- What an intranet is and the differences between intranets and the Internet or World Wide Web (WWW).

- How to navigate through an intranet to get the information you need.

- How to use two of the most widely used navigation tools (browsers)—Netscape Navigator and Microsoft Internet Explorer—to access your company's intranet.

- How to personalize and use these browsers based on your job and interests.

As you read and use this book, there are two important points to remember:

1. All discussion and examples assume a Windows 95 environment. However, if you are not using Windows 95, the concepts presented are still valid in other operating environments.

2. Every company uses intranets differently. Your intranet will not necessarily look like the examples herein. Use these examples to understand typical functions and uses, and to build your comfort level with the technology.

# How To Use This Book

This book is divided into three parts. Part 1, "What Is an Intranet?" (Lessons 1-3), introduces the concepts of an intranet and provides some background and perspective on the technology. Part 2, "Using an Intranet" (Lessons 4-21), provides step-by-step examples on how to use important intranet features and functions, including the two most popular browsers. Using electronic mail is also covered in this part. Part 3, "Moving Beyond Corporate Boundaries" (Lesson 22), presents information on emerging intranet capabilities and issues involved in connecting to the Internet, such as security and "firewalls."

# Conventions Used in This Book

You'll find icons throughout this book to help you save time and learn important information fast:

**Timesaver Tips** These give you insider hints and short-cuts for using an intranet in relation to Windows 95.

 **Plain English** These icons call your attention to definitions of new terms.

 **Panic Button** Look to these icons for warnings and cautions about potential problem areas.

You'll also find common conventions for steps you will perform:

| | |
|---|---|
| **What you type** | Things you type will appear in bold, color type. |
| Press Enter | Any keys you press or items you select with your mouse will appear in color type. |
| **On-screen text** | Any on-screen messages you see will appear in bold type. |
| Press Alt+F1 | Any key combinations you must press simultaneously will appear in this format. |
| URLs | Addresses appear in bold, color type. |
| **Names of fields and areas** | Names of fields and areas on-screen appear in bold in places where you are directed to them. |

# ABOUT THE AUTHORS

MBR Consulting, Inc., an Auctor Company, assists clients in improving productivity through the effective use of Information Systems Technology. Services provided span business-process analysis and requirements definition, technology acquisition and deployment, change management, and training and performance support. Internet/intranet consulting and development is a specialty. Clients range from small businesses to large multinational organizations.

# ACKNOWLEDGMENTS

MBR Consulting, Inc. appreciates the extraordinary efforts by all its employees to bring this book to print. A special thanks to Bill Christensen, Jodi Culp, Ralph Hoggard, Dan Meece, Bob Orr, Karen Reynolds, Lou Schmitt, Rhonda Tamulonis, and David Vasileff. Thanks also to the Que personnel for their guidance and patience.

# TRADEMARKS

All terms mentioned in this book that are known to be trademarks have been appropriately capitalized. Que Corporation cannot attest to the accuracy of this information. Use of a term in this book should not be regarded as affecting the validity of any trademark or service mark.

# Part 1

## WHAT IS AN INTRANET?

# INTRANETS ORIGINS AND USES

*In this lesson, you learn what intranets are, their relationship to the Internet, how they are used in corporations, and their effect on all software characteristics.*

## WHAT IS AN INTRANET?

Simply speaking, *intranet* is the term for the use of Internet and World Wide Web (WWW) technology on an internal network. Just as the Internet connects and makes information easily accessible from networks and computers in companies, businesses, governments, and schools around the world, an intranet can connect and make accessible the islands of information on separate computers within an organization.

The technology involves standards, protocols, tools, and languages that are simple, consistent, and easy to use. There will be more information about this topic in the next lesson. Just remember that you can think of an intranet as Internet-like capabilities on a corporate or internal network. This means that from a graphical user interface, you can point and click your way to the information you need just as you do now with the Windows 95 help system.

Many readers already know the drill: click a highlighted word or graphical image (called a *link*), or a button, and go to different screens (pages) of information; go forward or backward among pages by clicking the arrow buttons at the top of the screen. It's that easy to get started using an intranet.

# HOW AND WHY CORPORATIONS ARE USING INTRANETS

**Web Site**   A computer on your network that manages and transmits information on your intranet.

Observing the explosive growth of information being added to the Internet and particularly the WWW, companies began to consider establishing their own intranets or internal *Web sites*. These intranets could address a major information systems problem that had been around since mainframes and terminals—disseminating timely and consistent information to a broad audience in a cost-effective manner. Intranets are comparatively inexpensive, flexible, hardware platform-independent, simple, and easy to use. These attributes make a compelling case for intranets to solve this information-systems problem.

**Web Page**   A unit or block of text and graphical information, like a page in a book, displayed on your PC when you access your Intranet.

For example, human resource departments collect, maintain, and publish mountains of paper about policies, benefits, and regulations. Keeping this information current, updated, and in the hands of employees is nearly impossible in most organizations. At any given time, some employees will have erroneous or outdated information in their handbooks. Maintaining this same information on an internal Web site and making it available to all employees on an intranet, instead of printing it, is an elegant solution. Since there really is only one copy, it is much simpler for human resources to keep it updated; and employees who access the information by pointing and clicking hyperlinks on their intranet *Web pages* are guaranteed to get the latest information.

Human resource applications are but one example of hundreds of good uses for intranets within companies. Sales, marketing, engineering, customer service, and research departments all have equally compelling reasons to use intranets to solve similar problems. At Compaq Computer, for example, employees access and change 401(k) plans via an intranet. At Ford, engineers worldwide communicate and collaborate on automobile design.

Federal Express has been innovative in its use of intranet technology. For years, customers called agents by phone to look up package delivery status on terminals connected to mainframes. As technology advanced, agents were given intranet technology to more easily access information to answer customer inquiries. Recently, this same intranet system was made available on the Internet so that customers can check the status of shipments themselves without human intervention. Figure 1.1 displays the inquiry screen. Figure 1.2 displays the results of entering an airbill number.

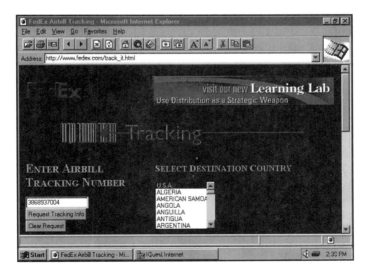

FIGURE 1.1    An inquiry screen.

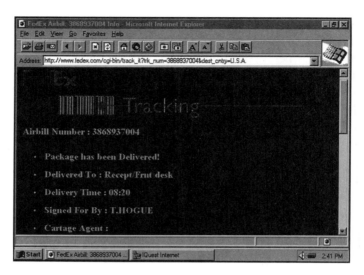

FIGURE 1.2    Entering an airbill number.

This is an excellent example of corporate use of an intranet, which has evolved to even wider usage. Customers like the easy access, and Federal Express has saved lots of money. Because of this success, over 50 Web sites are now running inside Federal Express—most for use by employees.

Publishing information is the most commonplace use of intranets today, but many other applications are emerging (see Lesson 21). One of the more interesting aspects is the growing ability for several users to collaborate on the same document.

## INTRANETS: EFFECT ON TRADITIONAL SOFTWARE

Many traditional providers of application software solutions are beginning to feel the squeeze from intranet-available features and functions.

Lotus Notes is a good example of the rapidly changing software marketplace. Notes, the current market leader for collaborative software or *groupware*, offers features and functions (such as version control, document check-in/check-out, and so on) not inherently present in intranet technology. But many new software vendors are introducing products that will add Notes-type functions to work in an intranet environment. At the same time, Lotus is adapting its products for closer integration with Web use.

The future? Who knows? The environment is dynamic. Most likely, similar to the above example, existing software products will evolve to coexist with and take advantage of Web technology and new products that expand applicability will continue to be introduced. The basic intranet or Web infrastructure will become so widely used that it will be taken for granted in software products. You will learn about these emerging intranet capabilities in Lesson 21.

In this lesson, you learned where intranets originated, how they are currently being used by some companies, and what the future might hold. In the next lesson, you will learn about all the hardware and software that is necessary for running an intranet.

# WHAT MAKES UP AN INTRANET?

*In this lesson, you learn what is required to have an intranet and the definition of major components.*

**Talking the Talk**   You don't need to memorize all the terms and concepts in this lesson before you can use an intranet. However, such an understanding may make succeeding lessons more meaningful, and in a lot of jobs it may be important to "talk the talk."

## INTRANETS: THE BIG PICTURE

**Local Area Network (LAN)**   Refers to end-user PCs connected to a common system within the same physical facility.

As mentioned in Lesson 1, intranets are essentially Internet or Web technology running on an internal corporate network. Although how a company's network and intranet is set up, or *configured,* and maintained is the responsibility of the Network Administrator (and beyond the scope of this book), it's important to understand, in a general way, the hardware and software pieces, or components, that make up an intranet. Figure 2.1 is an example of a simple intranet *configuration* on a small corporate Local Area Network (LAN).

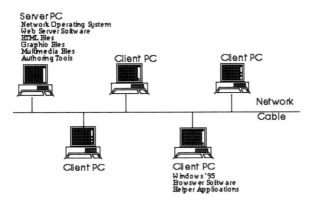

**FIGURE 2.1** An example of an intranet.

# INTRANETS: THE DETAILED PICTURE

Table 2.1 defines all the hardware and software components that comprise an intranet, as shown in Figure 2.1:

**TABLE 2.1 INTRANET COMPONENTS**

| COMPONENT | DESCRIPTION |
|---|---|
| Server PC | The PC or workstation that stores all applications and Web pages. The end users will access the server PC to bring the intranet information to their PCs. |
| Client PC | The end user's PC, used to access the intranet information stored on the server PC. |
| Network | System level software that controls a Operating System PC's most basic functions and allows other PCs in a network to communicate. |
| Web Server | Software running on the server that stores, manages, and updates HTML files and communicates with other programs. |

*continues*

TABLE 2.1    CONTINUED

| COMPONENT | DESCRIPTION |
| --- | --- |
| HTML (HyperText Markup Language) | HyperText is text that contains links to other information. HTML is the programming language that controls the appearance and behavior of information displayed on an intranet. |
| Authoring Tools | Software that facilitates the creation of pages in HTML. |
| Multimedia Files | Files containing sound and/or video. |
| Graphic Files | Files containing images or pictures. |
| Browsers | Software running on a client PC used to access and display HTML files on Web sites. |
| Helper Applications | Add-on or complimentary software that expands browser capabilities. A typical helper application could display a particular type of graphics or multimedia file that the browser would not otherwise be able to process. |

# PUTTING IT ALL TOGETHER

Now we can expand our definition of an intranet. An intranet consists of two basic components:

1. A Web server running on an internal corporate network that controls and manages intranet files.

2. Viewing tools, such as a browser and helper applications, running on a client PC that allow the end user to view and interact with intranet information.

In this lesson, you learned the concepts and definitions that prepare you to begin to explore your corporate intranet. In the next lesson, you will learn how to access your intranet.

# PREPARING TO ACCESS THE INTRANET

*In this lesson, you learn how to get ready to access an intranet.*

## YOUR USER ID AND PASSWORD

**Wide Area Network (WAN)**   Refers to users connected to a common system from different physical facilities.

The first step in accessing your company's intranet is to log on to your company's Local Area Network (LAN) or Wide Area Network (WAN). As you probably know, each company has its own unique way of identifying its network users through a series of user IDs and passwords. Although this maze seems burdensome to employees anxious to get to work on their LAN, it is necessary to protect the company's data from unauthorized access.

**What's the Password?**   If you do not have the requisite username and password and the related log-on procedures, you should contact your system administrator or corporate help desk for these details. Once you have this information, you are ready to access your company's LAN.

# LOGGING ON TO YOUR COMPANY'S NETWORK

As discussed in the Introduction, this book assumes your computer is running Windows 95 and that you know how to connect to the network. This is good news for you—you don't have to memorize any confusing and cumbersome DOS commands to start using your software.

When you turn your computer on, several internal tests are performed to determine whether your hardware and software are functioning properly. After the completion of these tests, Windows 95 automatically retrieves information about the normal user of that PC. It verifies three questions:

1. Is this computer connected to a LAN or WAN?

2. Who is the normal user of this PC?

3. What will the desktop look like?

After retrieving this information, Windows 95 opens the Enter Network Password dialog box and requests your password. Your computer should have the username of the verified normal user inserted in the appropriate box. If you are accessing the LAN from someone else's computer, you will need to change the username to your own.

Now just type your password in the Password text box. You won't see any characters as you type. This feature prevents unauthorized access to your LAN and Intranet.

 **TIP**  **Getting It Right**  Windows 95 puts an asterisk in the Password text box for each letter or number you type, so you know whether you entered the right number of characters.

Now press Enter or click OK. If you typed your password correctly, you're on the LAN. If not, Windows 95 lets you know and gives you another chance.

**ACCESS DENIED!**   You just sat down and tried to access your files from someone else's computer and got the message **ACCESS DENIED**. This is because each computer, user name, and password combination has been set to protect proprietary data. Simply arrange to log off the other employee's computer and log back on using your own user name and password. You can now access your own information.

## Accessing the Company Network While You Travel

Our society is becoming more mobile every day. People are finding ways to be on the move but still in contact with their offices. Cellular phones make it easier for travelers to check in or to call that important customer while driving on the interstate.

With a portable computer, cellular phone, and cellular-enabled modem, you could even access your company's LAN from your car. (For safety's sake, it's best if the car is stationary!) The same tools allow you access from locations like a hotel room or a sunny beach. Even better, you can probably access your LAN and your intranet information 24 hours a day, seven days a week.

Most organizations have the ability to access their LANs from remote sites using a dial-up capability. Thus, if you can access your company's LAN from across the street, you can access your company's intranet from around the world. You only need a few tools to access your company's LAN from the road—a laptop computer with a high speed modem, a communications software package, and a telephone line. You can connect your laptop to the LAN over the telephone lines.

**Reduce Phone Bills!** If your company doesn't already have an 800 number set up to receive incoming LAN connections, you might suggest one. Whenever you connect to the LAN over phone lines, you're charged for an ongoing long distance call.

Before you travel, check with your system administrator to determine the specific procedures and hardware/software requirements regarding if, and how, you can access your company's LAN from somewhere outside your office.

## Using Web Browsers to Access the Company Intranet

Now, armed with your username, password, and logon procedures, whether you are at your desk or on the road, you are ready to access your company's intranet information. A browser is the only tool that will allow you to do so. Without a browser, all you'll see is a jumble of codes.

**Browser** Software that translates HTML or other intranet languages and presents the information in the form of graphics, audio presentations, full-motion videos, or simple text.

Two of the most popular web browsers are Netscape Navigator and Internet Explorer. In fact, right now, sales of these two browsers comprise the majority of the browser marker. Accessing your browser is generally as easy as double-clicking an icon such as those shown following this paragraph. Your system administrator might have created a custom icon to represent your browser which might look different than the ones shown here.

Netscape Navigator Browser

Microsoft Internet Explorer Browser

The Internet

If your company does not utilize icons for accessing a browser, you may also access it by other means. These access options will be discussed in detail in Lessons 4 and 11. Once you have determined which of these browsers your company is using, you can reference the appropriate lessons for your browser. Information about Netscape Navigator is provided in Lessons 4-10. Internet Explorer is discussed in Lessons 11-17.

In this lesson, you learned about your user ID and password. You also learned how to log on to your company's network. In the next lesson, you learn basic information about the Netscape browser.

# Part 2

## Using an Intranet

# NETSCAPE 2.0 BROWSER BASICS

*In this lesson, you learn how to open*
*and close your Netscape browser, and about the Netscape screen.*

## ABOUT THE NETSCAPE BROWSER

Although the Netscape browser was originally designed for browsing the Internet, it is equally applicable for use on your company's intranet.

As mentioned in Lesson 2, there is a special language for handling information on an intranet—HTML (HyperText Markup Language). HTML is the universal computer language of the World Wide Web. However, you don't really need to understand HTML because Netscape does the work for you. As you browse through information on your intranet, Netscape translates HTML codes and presents the resulting information for your viewing pleasure. You may see graphics, listen to audio presentations, view full motion video, or simply read some text.

## OPENING THE NETSCAPE BROWSER

If your system administrator has set up a Netscape shortcut icon on your desktop, just double click it to start Netscape. If you do not have an icon to access this browser, follow the standard steps for running a Windows 95 program as follows:

 **Remember!** Don't forget that you need to be connected to your network in order to access intranet information with your browser.

To open the Netscape 2.0 browser, follow these steps:

**1.** Click the Start button on the Windows 95 Taskbar. The Start menu opens, as shown in Figure 4.1.

**Figure 4.1**   Starting Netscape.

   **Icon Shortcuts**   The Taskbar is located at the bottom of your screen in Windows 95. Use it to restore minimized applications or open new programs on your desktop.

**2.** Choose Programs to open the Programs menu.

**3.** Choose Netscape to open the Netscape menu and click Netscape to start the Netscape browser.

   **Remember!**   You may need a user ID and password to access your intranet via Netscape.

**4.** Netscape starts, and your intranet home page is displayed, as shown in Figure 4.2.

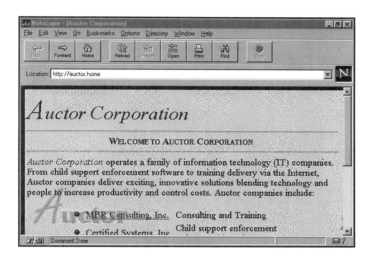

**FIGURE 4.2**    The Netscape browser screen.

 **Where's My Home Page?**    If you start Netscape and your intranet's home page does not appear, it's possible you're not properly connected to your intranet or a browser setting is incorrect. Contact your system administrator if this happens. (More information on home pages is provided in Lesson 5.)

# UNDERSTANDING THE NETSCAPE BROWSER SCREEN

Like other Windows applications, Netscape has an essential set of features that enable you to quickly navigate through your intranet. Figure 4.3 shows these important features, and Table 4.1 defines them further.

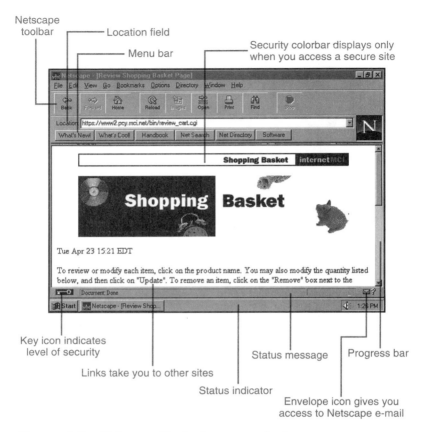

Netscape
toolbar ——————— Location field

———— Menu bar

Security colorbar displays only
when you access a secure site

Key icon indicates
level of security

Status message    Progress bar

Links take you to other sites

Status indicator

Envelope icon gives you
access to Netscape e-mail

**FIGURE 4.3**   Netscape Navigator screen features.

**TABLE 4.1   NAVIGATOR SCREEN FEATURE DESCRIPTIONS**

| SCREEN | FEATURE OPERATION |
| --- | --- |
| Menu Bar | Displays drop-down menu items specific to Netscape and similar to other Windows 95 applications. |

*continues*

TABLE **4.1**    CONTINUED

| SCREEN | FEATURE OPERATION |
| --- | --- |
| Netscape Toolbar | Displays icons for the most commonly used Netscape commands, which help in finding and using intranet information. |
| Location Field | Displays the location or URL (full path and file name) of the Web page you are viewing. |
| Status Indicator | Displays meteors streaking by the "N" in the Netscape logo to indicate in-process activity. This activity may include loading a page or graphics. |
| Security Colorbars | Differentiate between secure and unsecure pages. Blue bars indicate a secure page. Gray bars indicate no security. Most of the bars you see will be gray. |
| Links | Denotes a hyperlink from the current words or graphic to another page or document. Links are usually indicated by a different color and/or underlined text. |
| Security Indicator | The key icon shows the security level of the page you are viewing. A solid, highlighted key denotes a high level security. A broken key represents a low or no security level. |
| Status Message | Shows the current URL and important messages specific to Netscape. These are usually links to other pages or computers. |
| Progress Bar | Displays a colored bar that slides from left to right to depict Netscape's progress in accessing or loading a page. |

TABLE 4.1  CONTINUED

| SCREEN | FEATURE OPERATION |
| --- | --- |
| Netscape Mail | The envelope icon gives you access to Netscape's e-mail function. |

# EXITING NETSCAPE

You can exit Netscape by using one of the following methods:

- Open the File menu, as shown in Figure 4.4. Click Close or Exit. Exit will close all open windows in Netscape. Close will only close the active window; any other open Netscape window will remain open.

- Click the Close (X) button in the upper-right corner of the window (see Figure 4.4).

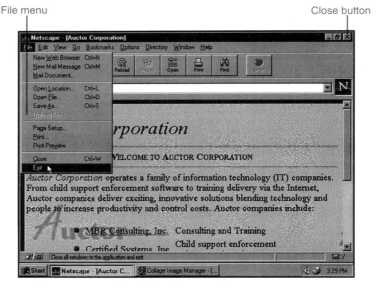

FIGURE 4.4    Exiting the Netscape browser.

In this lesson, you learned how to open and exit Netscape. You also learned the different features on the Netscape browser screen.

In the next lesson, you learn how to access and change your company's home page, use links within pages, and use the Open function.

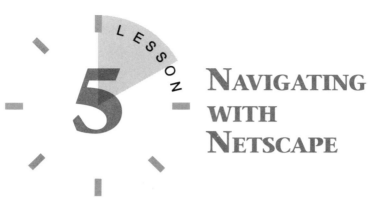

# NAVIGATING WITH NETSCAPE

*In this lesson, you learn how to access your home page, use links, use the toolbar, use the "Open" function, and change your home page.*

## WHAT IS NAVIGATING?

Now that you have an understanding of the basics of Netscape 2.0 and how an intranet is constructed, you are probably eager to get started looking at the information on your intranet. That's what this chapter is all about. You learn ways to move among the pages of information on your intranet. This moving from page to page is called *navigating*.

**Page**   A page of information on your intranet is just like a page in a book. It is one block of information displayed on your browser screen for you to read. Pages can contain both text and graphics, and you may need to scroll to see the entire page. Each page is stored in a file on a server on your intranet.

## ACCESSING THE HOME PAGE

When you start Netscape, a page will automatically be displayed. This page is called the home page and is set up by your system administrator. This could be a company, department, or personal home page. There's nothing sacred about a home page. It is simply the starting point for further navigation. At some point you may even want to change your home page to one that's a more useful starting point for you. The last section of this lesson shows you how to change your home page.

# USING LINKS

From your home page or any other page, you can move to and look at other pages using a feature called *links*. When you pass your mouse pointer over a link, it automatically changes to a hand symbol, as shown in Figure 5.1. Click a link to go from viewing the current page to viewing a different page. This process will sometimes be referred to as "following links."

Netscape toolbar

Link

**FIGURE 5.1**    The hand symbol identifies a link.

**Links**    A link connects one intranet page to another. Links are identified by colored and/or underlined text or graphics. This type of connection is called hypertext.

Take a few minutes and practice following links on pages on your intranet. Notice that after you follow a link, it changes to a different color.

# Using the Toolbar

After you've linked from page to page several times, it's not uncommon to fq8Áet how you got to where you are. You may get to a page and want to reread the one you just came from, or you may want to get back to your home page to follow another set of links. The designers of Netscape Navigator anticipated these requirements and provided a simple way to do all of the above and some other frequently used functions. They designed a toolbar with icons that allow these tasks to be accomplished with little more than the click of a mouse (see Figure 5.1).

Table 5.1 provides a brief explanation of what happens when you click each button on the toolbar.

**Table 5.1    Toolbar Functions**

| Icon | Icon Name | Description |
|------|-----------|-------------|
| Back | Back | Takes you back to the previous page. For example, if you click Back three times, Netscape will display the last three pages you viewed. If you haven't moved from your home page, this button is grayed and cannot be used. |
| Forward | Forward | Takes you to the page that was displayed before you clicked the Back button. This button is dependent on whether you have used the Back button. |
| Home | Home | Takes you to your home page. |

*continues*

**Table 5.1 Continued**

| Icon | Icon Name | Description |
|---|---|---|
| | Reload | Reloads and displays the current page again. You'll only use this button if the page you're viewing has changed since the last time you loaded it or if there is a problem with the loaded page. |
| | Images | If Netscape is set to display text without images, clicking this button will cause the corresponding images to be displayed as well. |
| | Open | Allows you to enter an intranet address (URL) that you desire to access. |
| | Print | Prints a copy of the current page. |
| | Find | Allows you to find every occurrence where a word or phrase appears on a page. |
| | Stop | Allows you to cancel the loading process, whether contacting a new Web site, loading a new Web page or displaying graphics. |

# Using the Open Location Function

Sometimes you may want to visit a page that is not directly linked to your home page or any other page that you can access by links. Perhaps a coworker tells you about a page and gives you its location.

Netscape can easily link to any page on your intranet, but its address or location must be communicated to Netscape in a special and exact format. Page locations in this special format are called

Uniform Resource Locators (URL). If you aren't used to them, URLs look like gibberish with dots and dashes thrown in. Here's an example of a URL: **http://AUCTOR.COM/MBR/ HIST.HTML**.

 **On the Case**   URLs are case sensitive, so be careful. **TIP**   The hardest thing about URLs is entering them without typos!

So what does the gibberish mean? You don't really need to know how to use URLs, but in case you're interested:

**TABLE 5.2   PARTS OF A URL**

| URL | OPERATION |
| --- | --- |
| **http://** | Indicates a hypertext page is the destination of the link. |
| **AUCTOR.COM** | Indicates the name of the computer the page is on. |
| **/MBR/** | Indicates the directory or folder the page is in. |
| **HIST.HTML** | Provides the actual file name of the page. (Sometimes the .HTML is omitted.) |

URLs can be vital to accessing Web pages. If you do not have a link to a page, the only way to access it is to enter its URL. The following steps show you how to enter the URL of a page you want to access. This is called Opening a Location.

1. On the Menu bar, open the File menu and click Open Location, or click on the Open button on the Netscape toolbar. The Open Location dialog box appears, as shown in Figure 5.2.

**FIGURE 5.2** The Open Location dialog box.

**2.** Type the URL of the page you want to see.

**Path-ology** The composition of a URL may differ based on the structure of your intranet. For example, the extension .HTML may be shortened to .HTM or you may not need to use the extension at all. So, don't be surprised if your URLs look different from the ones you see referenced in this book.

**3.** Click the Open button or press the Enter key on your keyboard. The page you desire is displayed.

**A Quick URL Trip** You can also access your desired page by typing the URL in the location field. You will note that the field name becomes "Go to." Hit enter and the desired page will be displayed.

# How to Reset Your Home Page

After you browse, link, and navigate for a while, you may find that the home page that was set as a default is not as good a starting point for your use as another page, and you'd like to have that page display automatically when you start Netscape. In other words, you want to change your home page.

You will need to write down the URL of the page you want to make your new home page before you follow the steps below. If

you haven't written it down or can't remember it exactly, go to it
and write the URL down now (see Figure 5.3).

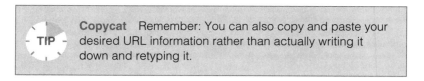

> **Copycat**  Remember: You can also copy and paste your
> desired URL information rather than actually writing it
> down and retyping it.

URL of New Home Page

**Figure 5.3**    URL of desired new home page.

1. Click Options on the menu bar and click General Preferences in the drop-down menu. The Preferences dialog box
   appears, as shown in Figure 5.4

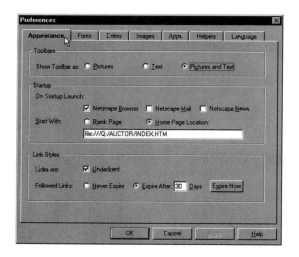

**Figure 5.4**    The Preferences dialog box.

2. If not already displayed, click the Appearance tab.

**3.** In the Startup area, ensure that the Netscape browser option is checked. If not, click it.

**In the Beginning**   Whatever you select in the Startup area will be the window that is displayed when you access Netscape. The most common option to select is the Netscape browser. If you choose Netscape Mail, Netscape's e-mail option will be the only window displayed when you start.

**4.** Under the Start With option, click the Home Page Location option.

**5.** Delete the information currently showing in the text box below the Start With options.

**6.** Enter the URL of the page you want as your new home page into the text box.

**7.** Verify that you have entered the correct information, and click the OK button.

**8.** The dialog box disappears and you return to the page you were in before accessing the General Preferences option.

**9.** Click the home button to verify that you have entered the URL of your desired new home page.

In this lesson, you learned how to navigate in the Netscape Browser, using the links, the toolbar, and the Open function; and you learned how to change your home page. In the next lesson, you learn how to add, view, and delete bookmarks.

# 6 SETTING BOOKMARKS IN NETSCAPE

*In this lesson, you learn to add, view, and delete bookmarks.*

## UNDERSTANDING BOOKMARKS

As you explore your intranet, you may come across some helpful pages that you'd like to revisit without having to remember how you got there. Netscape has a useful way of helping you remember pages you want to revisit: you can *bookmark* them. A Netscape bookmark remembers the URL of a page, its name, the date you added this particular page to your bookmark list, and the last time you visited the page—all useful information to help you quickly locate a page you want to reread.

## ADDING BOOKMARKS

In order for Netscape to remember bookmarks, you must add them to the bookmark list. That way, the next time you want to return to the bookmarked page, you can select its name from a menu at the top of the Netscape window, and you will automatically be taken to that page.

To add a bookmark, follow these steps:

1. Go to the page you want to save as a bookmark.

2. Open the Bookmarks menu.

3. Select the Add Bookmark command (see Figure 6.1).

**FIGURE 6.1**    The Bookmarks menu's Add Bookmark command.

**4.** The page is now added to the bottom of the Bookmarks menu, which you can see when you open that menu (see Figure 6.2).

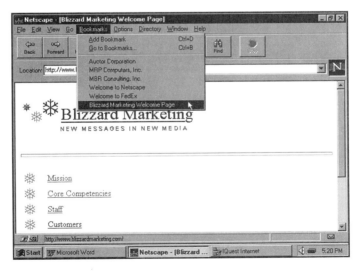

**FIGURE 6.2**    The Bookmarks menu after you add the new bookmark.

# MINIMIZING BOOKMARKS

As you surf your intranet, you may find it helpful to have the bookmark.htm window minimized for easy access. This keeps you from having to open the Bookmarks menu each time you want to view a bookmarked page.

If you want to minimize the bookmark.htm window and access your bookmarks without opening the Bookmarks menu, follow these steps:

1. Open the Bookmarks menu.

2. Click on the Go to Bookmarks... option.

3. A window labeled **Bookmarks-bookmark.htm** appears, which contains a hierarchical listing of all the pages you bookmarked (see Figure 6.3).

 **TIP**    **Bookmark.htm**    As you create your Bookmarks list, Netscape creates a new Web page to hold links to these pages. The file for that Web page is called bookmark.htm.

4. Click on the Minimize button in the Bookmarks window.

 **TIP**    **More Ways to Get There**    You also have two alternative methods to hide your bookmarks window. 1) Double-click one of these bookmarks. The Bookmarks window disappears behind your Netscape window. The Web page that you bookmarked displays in the Netscape window. 2) Click anywhere on the Netscape window to make it the active window and hide your Bookmarks window behind it.

5. Notice that the Bookmarks window is now an icon displayed on your task bar.

The Bookmarks window                         The Minimize button

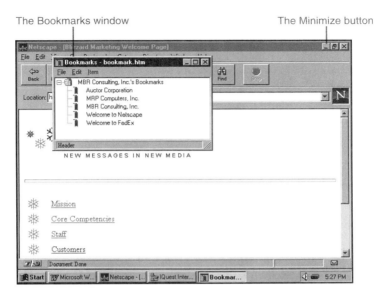

**Figure 6.3**    The Bookmarks window appears on top of the main Netscape window.

6.  To restore your Bookmarks window, click once on the Bookmarks icon located on the task bar.

7.  To completely close the Bookmarks window, open the File menu and select Close.

# Deleting Bookmarks

As you add bookmarks, you may bookmark a page by accident, or you may decide a bookmarked page is no longer useful. In these cases, you will want to delete the bookmark from your list to make space for more useful bookmarks.

To delete a bookmark that you no longer want, follow these steps:

1.  Open the Bookmarks menu.

2.  Click Go to Bookmarks.

3.  As illustrated in Figure 6.4, the Bookmarks-bookmark.htm window displays, containing your bookmarks.

**4.** Click the bookmark that you want to delete. The bookmark is then highlighted.

**Figure 6.4**    The Bookmark window with the bookmark highlighted.

**5.** Press the Delete key to delete the highlighted bookmark.

**6.** To close the Bookmarks-bookmark.htm window, open the File menu and click Close.

**Come Back, Little Bookmark!**   If you accidentally delete a bookmark, you can get it back by immediately selecting Undo from the Edit menu in the Bookmarks window.

In this lesson you learned how to add, view, and delete bookmarks in Netscape. In the next lesson, you learn how to organize and edit your bookmarks.

# ORGANIZING AND MOVING BOOKMARKS

*In this lesson, you learn how to organize and move bookmarks.*

## ORGANIZING BOOKMARKS INTO AN ORDERED LIST

As you continue surfing your company's intranet, you will want to add more bookmarks for easy reference. As you know, when you add a bookmark, Netscape simply appends it to the end of your bookmark list. Over time, your bookmark list may become quite lengthy, and you may want to change its sequence.

There are various ways to organize your bookmarks into a meaningful list. Some people organize their bookmarks alphabetically, others by frequency of access. No matter what way you choose, use the following steps to organize your bookmarks into an ordered list.

1. Open the Bookmarks menu.

2. For this example, make sure you have at least four bookmarks on your list. (To add bookmarks, refer to Lesson 6, "Setting Bookmarks in Netscape.")

3. With the Bookmarks menu open, click Go to Bookmarks.

4. The Bookmarks-bookmarks.htm window displays, as shown in Figure 7.1.

FIGURE 7.1    The Bookmarks-bookmarks.htm window.

**5.** Click the bookmark you want to move.

**6.** Open the Edit menu.

**7.** Click Cut.

**8.** Click the bookmark you would like to appear above the bookmark you're moving. For example, if you want to move the MBR Consulting bookmark so it displays under the Auctor Corporation bookmark, you need to click the Auctor Corporation bookmark.

**9.** On the Netscape Menu bar, open the Edit menu.

**10.** Click Paste. The bookmark appears in the desired position, as shown in Figure 7.2.

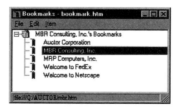

FIGURE 7.2    The bookmark moves to the desired location.

 **Shortcut!**    To quickly move a bookmark, simply drag and drop it in the new location.

# ADDING FOLDERS

As you organize your bookmarks, you might find it convenient to organize them even further than ordered lists. Netscape for Windows 95 gives you the ability to organize bookmarks into *folders*. This allows you to separate your bookmarks into logical groupings. For example, you might want to group your bookmarks by department, in which case you could set up folders for Human Resources, Marketing, Engineering, and so on, to contain bookmarks of pages of interest in each department. Use the following steps to add folders to your bookmark list.

1. On the Netscape Menu bar, open the Bookmarks menu.

2. For this example, make sure you have at least four bookmarks on your list. (To add bookmarks, refer to Lesson 6, "Setting Bookmarks in Netscape.")

3. With the Bookmarks menu open, click Go to Bookmarks. The Bookmarks-bookmarks.htm window displays (refer to Figure 7.1).

4. With the Bookmarks-bookmarks.htm window displayed, click the bookmark beneath which you would like the folder to appear.

5. Open the Item menu. Click Insert Folder.

6. The Bookmark Properties window displays with a tab labeled General, as shown in Figure 7.3.

7. In the Name field, type the name that you want the folder to have.

8. Press the Tab key on your keyboard to advance the cursor to the Description field. Type a brief description of what contents you plan to save in the folder.

9. Click OK. The window closes and returns you to the Bookmarks-bookmarks.htm window.

10. The folder is inserted in your list beneath the bookmark you highlighted in step four (see Figure 7.4).

FIGURE 7.3    The General tab in the Bookmark Properties window.

FIGURE 7.4    The inserted folder.

# MOVING BOOKMARKS INTO FOLDERS

Once you add folders to the Bookmarks-bookmarks.htm window, you will want to move some of your bookmarked items into the folders. Use the following steps to move bookmarked items into folders:

1.  Move a bookmark by dragging it to the folder you desire. You'll see the outline of the bookmark as you move it from one folder to another, as shown in Figure 7.5.

**What a Drag!**   To drag your bookmark, position your pointer on the bookmark you want to move. Click and hold the left mouse button. Move the mouse until the mouse pointer is where you want the bookmark to be placed, and then release the mouse button.

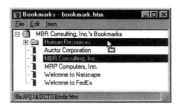

FIGURE 7.5   Dragging the bookmark.

2. Double click the folder to which you dragged the bookmark to see the saved bookmark inside it, as seen in Figure 7.6.

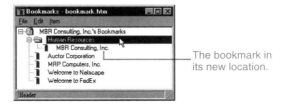

The bookmark in its new location.

FIGURE 7.6   A sample folder with saved bookmark inside.

**Are You Open?**   A plus (+) symbol next to a folder means that it is closed. Double clicking the folder will open it so you can view its contents. A minus (-) symbol next to a folder means that it is open. Double clicking the folder will close it when you no longer need to access the folder's contents.

In this lesson, you learned how to organize bookmarks in a list, create folders, and move bookmarks into folders. In the next lesson, you learn how to configure Netscape's appearance.

# CONFIGURING NETSCAPE APPEARANCE

*In this lesson, you learn how to change the look and feel of your intranet pages by changing the styles, fonts, colors, and images options.*

## CHANGING THE APPEARANCE OF THE NETSCAPE SCREEN

Once you start using the Netscape browser, you will probably want to customize the Netscape screen. You can do this from the Appearance tab in the Preferences dialog box.

For example, you can change the way Netscape displays its toolbars. The buttons on the toolbars can be displayed as pictures only, text only, or both picture and text.

Another option you have is to determine how you want your links to look. You can choose to have links displayed in a different color or underlined to clearly distinguish them from regular text in a Web page. Another option is to make links indistinguishable from other text except for the hand that appears when the cursor is over the link. (See Lesson 5.)

Finally, you can choose how long you want Netscape to "remember" the links you've already followed in any Web page, as addressed in Lesson 5. After you select a link it changes to a different color. Through Netscape preferences you can determine how long you want Netscape to remember these previously selected links. The normal amount of time that Netscape remembers your links is 30 days.

To change the look of the Netscape screen, follow these steps:

**1.** On the Menu bar, open the Options menu, then click General Preferences. The Preferences dialog box appears, as shown in Figure 8.1.

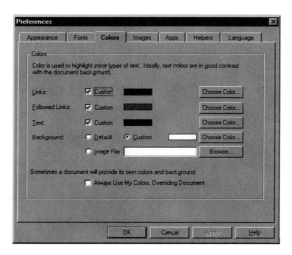

**FIGURE 8.1**    The Preferences dialog box.

**2.** If it is not displayed, click the Appearance tab to bring it to the front, as shown in Figure 8.2.

**3.** In the Toolbars section, you can display your Toolbar icons as pictures only, text only, or both. Click the option you want to select.

**4.** Under the Link Styles section, click the box beside the option you want to identify your links. For example, if you click on Underlined, your links will be underlined.

**5.** In the Followed Links section, click the circle beside Expire After:. This lets you choose how long Netscape will remember that you followed a specific link.

**6.** Click in the text box next to the Expire After: option and enter the number of days you want Netscape to keep the followed links.

**7.** Click OK to apply your changes and return to the Netscape screen.

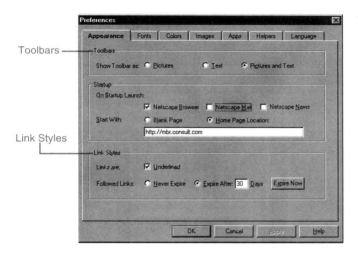

Toolbars

Link Styles

**FIGURE 8.2** The Appearance tab.

# CHANGING FONTS

Changing the fonts allows you to change the appearance of the text that is displayed in your intranet pages. This might be particularly helpful for those of us who don't see as well as we once did.

**Font**    Font describes the style and size of the text that is displayed on your Web pages. Many different sizes and styles are available to be displayed on your intranet.

To change font characteristics, follow these steps:

1. On the Menu bar, open the Options menu and click General Preferences. The Preferences dialog box appears.

2. In the Preferences dialog box, click the Font tab to display the Font dialog box, as shown in Figure 8.3.

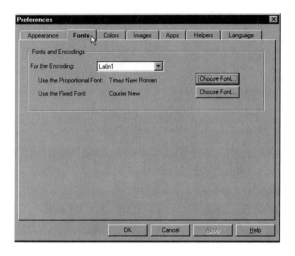

**FIGURE 8.3**    The Fonts tab.

3. To change the font face, click the Choose Font button. The Choose Base Font dialog box appears, as shown in Figure 8.4.

4. In the Font list, select the font type that you want. Use the scroll bars to view all the fonts that are not displayed. In the Size list, select the font size you want.

5. Click OK to close the Choose Base Font dialog box and return to the Preferences dialog box. Click OK to return to the Netscape screen.

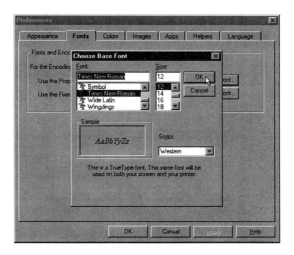

**FIGURE 8.4**    The Choose Base Font dialog box.

# CHANGING COLORS

Netscape allows you to choose the color of your links, followed links, text, and background of your intranet pages from the Colors tab in the Preferences dialog box.

To change the colors of the various Netscape screen elements, follow these steps.

1.  In the Preferences dialog box, click the Colors tab to display it, as shown in Figure 8.5.

2.  To change the default settings of any or all of these options, click the box beside the word Custom.

3.  Click the Choose Color button next to that option.

4.  A color palette appears, as shown in Figure 8.6.

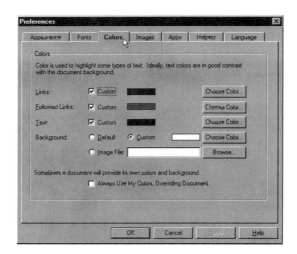

**FIGURE 8.5**    The Colors tab.

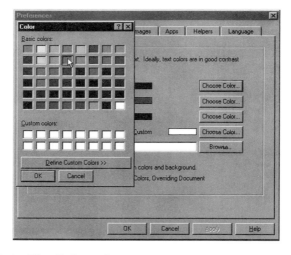

**FIGURE 8.6**    The Color palette.

**5.** Click the desired color square in the palette.

**6.** Click OK to close the color palette.

7. The color box will now show the new color you have chosen.

8. When you have chosen all of your colors, click OK to select your preferences and return to the Netscape screen.

**Fading Fast!**   Clicking the box at the bottom of the window labeled Always Use My Colors, Overriding Document will cause any of those pages with preestablished colors and backgrounds to lose their assigned colors. You may find this easier to read; however, recognize that you will lose the colors that were intended.

**Invisible Text!**   If, after you select your color preferences and return to the intranet, your text has disappeared, you probably chose a conflicting color scheme (such as a white background and white text). Repeat the steps to change back colors to your original color scheme.

## CHANGING IMAGES

Netscape can display intranet pages using your color monitor's capabilities in the *images* that are downloaded to the Netscape screen.

**Images**   Images are pictures or graphics displayed on a Web page.

Your monitor's display output may not have the capability to color the images exactly as they were originally created. Netscape provides options for compensating for this difference.

- **Automatic**   When this setting is selected, the image will be displayed using the most appropriate colors that your monitor has available. *Recommended*: Netscape's default setting.

- **Dither**   When this setting is selected, Netscape will use your monitor's colors to most closely match the original colors of the image. *Not recommended*: While providing the closest match, it takes longer to display.

- **Substitute Colors**   When this setting is selected, Netscape will substitute the colors that your monitor has available for colors in the original image. *Not recommended*: Not as close a match.

Also, you can control when Netscape loads images. Netscape provides the following options.

- **After Loading**   This setting will cause images to be displayed after the web page is loaded. *Recommended*: Will cause your pages to load more quickly on a high-speed connection like the intranet.

- **While Loading**   This setting will gradually load images. *Not recommended*: Will cause pages to load more slowly.

The following steps use the suggested settings.

1. In the Preferences dialog box, click the Images tab to display it, as shown in Figure 8.7.

2. Within the Choosing Colors area, click the circle beside Automatic.

3. Beside the Display Images option, click After Loading.

4. Click OK to return to your Netscape screen and continue working.

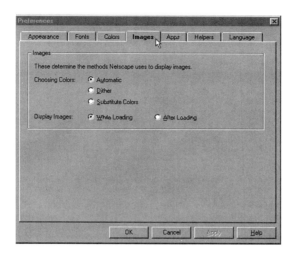

**FIGURE 8.7**   The Images tab.

In this lesson, you learned how to change the styles, fonts, text, colors and images of your intranet pages. In the next lesson, you will learn how to change the network options.

# CONFIGURING NETWORK PREFERENCES AND USING THE HISTORY FUNCTION

*In this lesson, you learn to configure Netscape network preferences options and use the History function.*

## CONFIGURING THE DOCUMENT CACHE OPTIONS

The first time you visit a Web page on your intranet, you may notice that it takes some time for it to completely display. Then, the next time you revisit that page, it seems to display almost instantaneously. This is due to a feature known as *cache*. Cache remembers Web pages that you have accessed and stores them locally on your PC. This feature eliminates the time it takes to reload a page from the network. Rather than loading the network version each time you visit a page, Netscape may load it from your cache.

Certain values in your cache are default values or have been set by your system administrator. The values for Memory Cache, Disk Cache, and Disk Cache Directory are default values and should not be changed. Your system administrator has probably set the size of your cache, and you most likely will not change this value.

**Cache** Cache is a storage area for Web pages that you have accessed on your intranet.

## CHANGING THE UPDATE PAGES DEFAULT

One of the options that you can change is how often your PC loads network pages during an intranet session. You have three options for controlling the frequency of retrieving information over the network.

**Verify documents once per session**   Selecting this option tells Netscape that you want to view the most current version of an intranet page. In this case, the network version of a page will always be retrieved the first time it is visited during any session on your intranet. Subsequent visits to that page in the same session will use the cached version. This option will give you the most current version of a page the first time you visit it in a session. This is the default setting, and the most commonly used option.

**Verify documents every time**   Selecting this option tells Netscape that you want to view the network version of a page each time that you visit it. Pages will not be loaded from cache if this option is selection. This option will always give you the most current version of a page; however, it will also take the most time to load pages.

**Verify documents never**   Selecting this option tells Netscape to always retrieve a desired page from your cache if it is available. In this case, Netscape will not automatically update to the most current version from the network; however, it will load your pages more quickly than the other options.

**Never Say Never**   Although the **Verify documents never** option will not load the most current intranet information automatically, a page can always be updated by using the Reload button. Clicking the Reload button will retrieve and display the network version of a page.

If you want to configure Netscape so that it doesn't automatically retrieve the network version of a document, follow these steps:

1. Open the Options menu and click the Network Preferences item. The Preferences window appears, as shown in Figure 9.1.

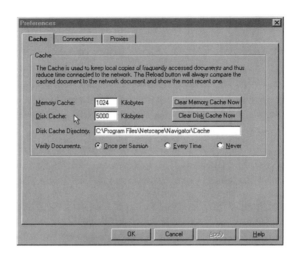

**FIGURE 9.1**   Preferences window.

2. Click the Cache tab. The option **Update Pages Once Per Session** is probably chosen.

3. Click the button beside the Never option, as shown in Figure 9.2.

4. Click the OK button to save the change and return to the current Web page.

**To Change or Not to Change?**   Most corporate networks have the power and capacity to transmit information quickly; therefore, you probably will not need to change your default settings unless you use a slower connection such as remote or dial-up access (see Lesson 3).

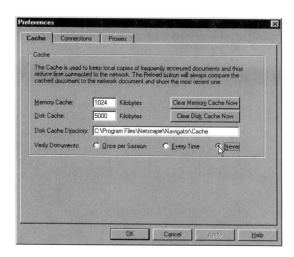

**FIGURE 9.2**   Clicking the Never option.

## CLEARING DOCUMENT CACHE

From time to time you may want to clear your document cache. As you continue to visit new pages and as changes occur to the existing pages, you may accumulate a lot of unnecessary and out-dated information. To clear Cache settings, follow these steps:

1. Open the Options menu and click the Network Preferences item.

2. Click the Cache tab. Your Cache options are displayed.

3. To clear the memory cache, click the Clear Memory Cache Now button. You will be prompted with a message as shown in Figure 9.3.

4. Clicking the OK button will remove all current files from the memory cache.

5. To clear disk cache, click the Clear Disk Cache Now button. You will be prompted with a message, as shown in Figure 9.4.

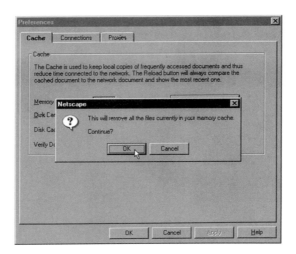

FIGURE 9.3   Clear Memory message.

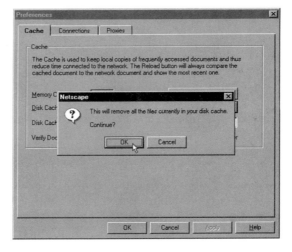

FIGURE 9.4   Clear Disk Cache message.

**6.** Click OK to remove all files from the disk cache memory.

**7.** Click OK to close the Preferences window and return to the current Web page.

# USING THE HISTORY FUNCTION

Every time you visit a new page or site, a Netscape feature keeps a log of these visits. This feature is called History, and it's a quick way to return to sites you've already visited. Each time you exit Netscape, this history will be erased.

Take the following steps to see how Netscape's History functions:

1. Bring up one of your favorite pages in your Intranet.

2. Using links, browse through several more pages.

3. After you have visited several more pages, click the Go menu. The history of the Web pages you just visited is located in the lower part of the Go menu, as shown in Figure 9.5.

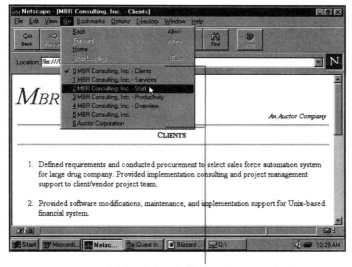

History is located below the separator bar.

FIGURE 9.5    Go Menu with pointer.

4. Once you have your History list in front of you, click one of the entries.

**5.** The selected page now appears in your browser.

**One-Track Mind**   Netscape's History function only tracks one thread. In other words, if you go back a few Web pages and then forward with a different set of links, the first pages you backed away from will be forgotten.

In this lesson, you learned how to change the network preferences options and use the history function in Netscape. In the next lesson, you learn the basics of Netscape e-mail.

# USING NETSCAPE E-MAIL

# 10

*In this lesson, you learn the basics of sending and receiving e-mail using Netscape.*

## WHAT IS E-MAIL?

E-mail is short for electronic mail. Basically, it is information addressed and transmitted over networks. Compared to regular mail, e-mail is very fast. There are many types of software for e-mail. The Netscape browser includes an easy-to-use e-mail capability.

In its simplest form, all e-mail has three parts:

1. The recipient's address, such as **mbr@auctor.com.**

2. The subject.

3. The content of the message.

Obviously, to send or receive e-mail, you must have an *address*. People who use the Internet to send e-mail probably know a recipient's address is usually the recipient's name or initials plus the Internet site separated by the @ sign. E-mail in Netscape via the intranet usually involves using the recipient's log-in name for the address. However, this configuration depends on how your mail administrator sets it up.

**TIP**

**Who Are You?** If you do not know your e-mail address, contact your mail administrator. This person may be different from your system administrator.

**No E-Mail?** Your mail administrator should have already configured Netscape's e-mail function. If Netscape's e-mail does not function properly—you are sending mail to users and they are not receiving it, or you cannot receive mail—contact your mail administrator.

# OPENING NETSCAPE E-MAIL AND VIEWING THE SCREEN

In order to access e-mail via Netscape, use the following steps:

1. Click the envelope icon in the bottom right corner of the Netscape window.

**Let Me in!** When you first access e-mail from Netscape, you may be required to enter your e-mail password. Once you have done so, Netscape will continue to grant you access until you completely exit Netscape.

2. The Netscape mailbox window appears, as shown in Figure 10.1. The title bar for this window may read differently depending on how your network is configured.

The parts of the Netscape Mail Window are explained in Table 10.1 and illustrated in Figure 10.1.

**TABLE 10.1   NETSCAPE MAIL PARTS**

| SCREEN PART | DESCRIPTION |
| --- | --- |
| Get Mail button | Retrieves from your communication server any messages that have been sent to you. Clicking this button is the equivalent of walking to your mailbox to pick up your mail. |

| | |
|---|---|
| Delete button | Sends a message to a trash folder. Your message isn't really deleted, and you can retrieve it, until you exit Netscape. When you exit Netscape, all messages are permanently deleted. |
| To: Mail button | Allows you to create a new message. |
| Inbox folder | Stores retrieved messages (saves mail you have received and read). |
| Trash folder | Stores deleted messages until you exit Netscape. |
| Sent folder | Stores a copy of all messages you have sent. |
| Message Display Area | Displays e-mail messages, including Sender, Subject, and Date of message. |

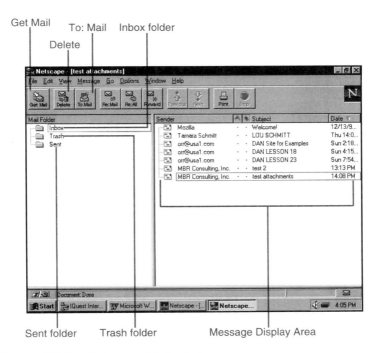

**FIGURE 10.1** Netscape Mail window.

# SENDING SIMPLE E-MAIL MESSAGES

What good is knowing how to access Netscape e-mail if you can't do anything with it? Fortunately, you can! Sending messages via e-mail is a quick and convenient way to relay information. Below are the steps for sending simple e-mail.

**TIP** **For Your Eyes Only?** Be aware that someone like the system or mail administrator can always read what is in mailboxes. The Electronic Privacy Act of 1986 provides some privacy guidelines; however, if you are writing something during regular work hours, the Act may not protect you from actions taken if you send something inappropriate in an e-mail message.

To send a simple e-mail message, follow these steps:

1. From the Netscape Mail window, click the To: Mail button or open the File menu and click New Mail Message.

2. The Message Composition window displays, as shown in Figure 10.2.

3. Type the recipient's e-mail address in the Mail To: field. Press the Tab key to advance to the next field.

4. If another individual needs to receive the message, type their e-mail address in the Cc: field to be carbon copied. Press the Tab key to advance to the next field.

5. Type the subject of the message in the Subject field. Press the Tab key to advance to the next field.

6. Type the message you want to send.

7. At the top left of the window, click the Send button.

8. The message is sent to the mail server and routed to the recipient(s) and the Netscape Message Composition window closes.

Sends the message

Address of the primary recipient

Address of secondary recipients

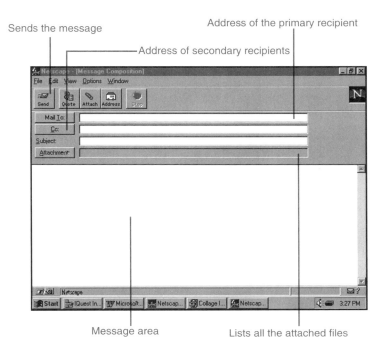

Message area

Lists all the attached files

**FIGURE 10.2**    Message Composition Window

**No Subject**    If you do not insert any text in the Subject field, a dialog box appears, stating **You did not specify a subject for this message. If you would like to provide one, please type it now.** You may type a subject in the field provided by the dialog box or **[no subject]** will be inserted. Choosing Cancel returns you to the Message Composition window. Choosing OK sends the message.

# ADDING ATTACHMENTS TO YOUR E-MAIL MESSAGE

When using e-mail, you may find it desirable to send documents created in other software applications, e-mail you saved as a file, or an intranet page along with your e-mail message. These items are known in Netscape as *attachments*.

> **Attachments**   Extra computer files that accompany the message portion of your e-mail. For example, an e-mail message might be, "Fred, I'm sending you the April sales report." An attachment might be a spreadsheet file containing the actual sales statistics.

## SENDING AN ATTACHED FILE

Attaching a file to an e-mail message is an efficient way to transmit information on your intranet. To accomplish these tasks, use the following steps:

> **You'll Have to Convert**   If the recipient does not have the same software that the file was created in, it must be converted to another format. For example, if you send an attachment that is a Microsoft Excel file and the recipient does not have Microsoft Excel on the receiving PC, the recipient is unable to use the Excel file.

1.  Prepare your e-mail message as in steps 1-6 in "Sending Simple E-Mail Messages."

2.  From the Netscape Message Composition window, locate the file you want to attach by using one of the following methods:

    • Open the File menu and click Attach File.

    • Click the Attach button at the top of the window.

3.  From the Attachments window, click the Attach File button. The Enter File to attach dialog box appears as shown in Figure 10.3.

FIGURE 10.3  The Enter file to attach dialog box.

**4.** Locate the file you wish to attach by clicking the down arrow next to the Look in text box.

**5.** Select the file and click Open.

**6.** The Attachments window opens and the file is attached and displayed, as shown in Figure 10.4.

FIGURE 10.4  File displayed in Attachments window.

**7.** Click OK. The Netscape Message Composition window appears (refer to Figure 10.2). The attached file name appears in the Attachment field.

**8.** Repeat this process as necessary to attach multiple files.

**9.** Now click the Send button as described in "Sending Simple E-Mail Messages" to send your message and any attached files.

## SENDING A URL (INTRANET) SITE AS AN ATTACHMENT

Different departments within your organization may have access to different intranet links and Web pages. You may want to send someone information from a Web page that they can't directly access through their own links. By attaching a URL to an e-mail message, you can communicate with them and provide them a copy of that intranet Web page.

Since you know how to send an e-mail message, you can easily attach a URL. To accomplish these tasks, use the following steps:

1. Prepare your e-mail message.

2. From the Attachments window (refer to Figure 10.4), click the Attach Location (URL) button. The Please Specify a Location to Attach window appears as shown in Figure 10.5.

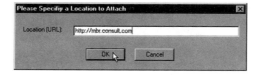

**FIGURE 10.5**    The Please Specify a Location to Attach window.

3. In the Please Specify a Location to Attach window, type the desired URL in the Location URL field.

4. Click OK.

5. The URL will appear in the Attachments window; click OK.

6. Repeat this process as necessary to attach multiple URLs.

7. Now click the Send button as described in "Sending Simple E-Mail Messages" to send your message and any attached URLs.

**Automatic Attachment**   If you only have one URL to send, go to that page. From there, select Mail Document from the Netscape File Menu. The URL of the current page will automatically be attached. Complete the message and send as normal.

# RETRIEVING YOUR E-MAIL

When others send you e-mail, it is stored in a PC called the mail server waiting for you to retrieve it. To retrieve e-mail messages, use the following steps:

1. If you're already in Netscape e-mail, skip to step 3. If not, click the envelope icon in the lower right corner of the Netscape window.

2. The Netscape mail window displays.

**New Mail Notification:**   Your mail administrator may have configured Netscape to check for new mail messages when you first open Netscape mail. If this occurs, a dialog box displays telling you whether you have new e-mail messages. You only need to check for new messages after you have been using e-mail for a certain period of time.

3. Click the Get Mail button at the top of the Netscape mail window or open the File menu and click Get New Mail (refer to Figure 10.1).

4. If there are no messages, a dialog box appears informing you that there are **No new messages on server.** If there are new messages, they will be located in your Inbox.

5. Click the Inbox folder to display a list of e-mail messages you have received (refer to Figure 10.1).

**6.** Click the e-mail message you want to read. The message, along with an attachment link (if any), will display in the bottom half of the Netscape mail window.

**What Is All This?!** Instead of getting an attachment link, I see the text from a file or a Web page in my e-mail message! The sender of the message has designated the attachment to be part of the e-mail message instead of a link to that attachment. Steps 7 and 8 will not apply.

**7.** To read the attached file, click the attachment link. The Save As... dialog box appears as shown in Figure 10.6.

**Figure 10.6**   The Save As... window.

**8.** Save the file to a drive and folder, as you would any other file. Now you can access the attached file as you would any other file, by opening it in the application in which it was created.

**Space Saver**   If you accumulate a large number of e-mail messages in any of your folders, Netscape mail may ask you to compress the mail folder the next time you start e-mail. Click OK to compress the messages; click Cancel to continue working without compressing.

# DELETING E-MAIL

When you start receiving e-mail, you will accumulate a number of messages in your Inbox. Eventually, you will want to delete some of these messages.

When you delete a message, it's not actually deleted until you completely exit Netscape or until you delete the file from within the Trash folder. If you haven't taken either of these actions, you can still retrieve the "deleted" message from the Trash folder. You can also move the deleted message from the Trash folder by dragging it to a different folder!

To delete an e-mail message, use the following steps:

1. From the Netscape e-mail window (refer to Figure 10.1), click the message in the Inbox that you want to delete.

2. Click the Delete button located on the toolbar.

3. The deleted message will now appear in the Trash folder (see Figure 10.7) and will be permanently deleted when you exit Netscape completely.

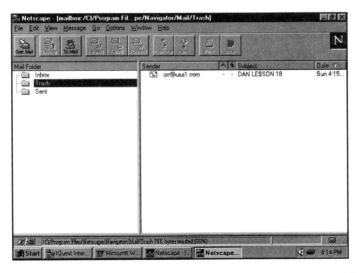

**FIGURE 10.7**    Open Trash folder with a deleted message inside.

In this lesson, you learned how to access Netscape e-mail, send
e-mail and attached documents, retrieve new e-mail messages,
and delete unwanted messages. In the next lesson you will learn
Internet Explorer basics. If you don't need to learn about Internet
Explorer, skip to Lesson 18.

# MICROSOFT INTERNET EXPLORER BASICS

*In this lesson, you learn how to start and exit the Microsoft Internet Explorer, about the Explorer window, and about the Help features.*

## ABOUT MICROSOFT INTERNET EXPLORER

Although Internet Explorer was designed for browsing the Internet, its concepts and principles can be applied to your company's Intranet.

Like Netscape, Microsoft Internet Explorer is a browser used to view documents on the World Wide Web and on your Intranet. Explorer is a software package that helps you use information on the Intranet. As mentioned in Lesson 2, there is a special language for handling information on an intranet—HTML (HyperText Markup Language). HTML is the universal computer language of the World Wide Web.

Now for some good news. You don't really need to understand HTML because Internet Explorer does the work for you. As you browse through information on your intranet, Explorer translates HTML codes and presents the resulting information for your viewing pleasure. You may see graphics, listen to audio presentations, view full motion video, or simply read some text.

## STARTING INTERNET EXPLORER

If you are connected to your company's LAN or WAN network, you are ready to access Internet Explorer whether in your office or

The Internet.

halfway across the world. (See "Accessing the Company Network While You Travel" in Lesson 3.) You can open the Internet Explorer browser in a couple of ways. First, you can simply double-click the icon called The Internet located on your desktop:

**TIP    Remember!** You may need a user ID and password to access your intranet via Internet Explorer.

**Interchangeable Icons** You notice that you don't have an Internet Explorer icon; instead, you have a different icon that indicates access to your intranet. Your system administrator may have installed a customized icon on your desktop for opening the Internet Explorer and accessing your intranet.

Or you can use the following steps:

1. Click the Start button on the Taskbar.

2. Choose Programs to open the Program menu.

3. Choose Accessories to open the Accessories menu.

4. Choose Internet Tools to open the Tools menu (see Figure 11.1).

5. Click Internet Explorer. Internet Explorer starts and your intranet home page is displayed.

**Where, Oh Where, Can It Be?** If you start Internet Explorer and your intranet's home page does not appear, you might not be properly connected to your intranet or a browser setting is incorrect. Contact your system administrator if this happens. (More information on home pages is provided in Lesson 12.)

**FIGURE 11.1**    Start/Programs/Accessories/Internet Explorer/
Internet Tools

# TOURING THE INTERNET EXPLORER WINDOW

Like other Windows 95 applications, Microsoft's Internet Explorer
has a useful set of window features designed to assist you in navigating through your intranet. Table 11.1 defines these features
and Figure 11.2 illustrates them.

**TABLE 11.1    INTERNET EXPLORER WINDOW FEATURE
DESCRIPTION**

| FEATURE | DESCRIPTION |
|---------|-------------|
| Toolbar | Displays icons for the most commonly used Internet Explorer commands, which help in finding and using intranet information. |

*continues*

**Table 11.1  Continued**

| Feature | Description |
| --- | --- |
| Menu bar | Displays drop-down menu items specific to Internet Explorer similar to other Windows 95 applications. |
| Minimize, Maximize (restore), and Close buttons | Function the same as in any Windows 95 application. |
| Title bar | Displays the title of the application as in all Windows 95 applications. |
| Address Field | Displays the location or URL (full path and file name) of the Web page you are viewing. |
| Status Indicator | Displays clouds racing past the Microsoft Windows logo to indicate in-process activity. This activity may include loading a page or graphics. |
| Progress Bar | Displays a colored bar that slides from left to right to depict Explorer's progress in accessing or loading files. |
| Status Message | Shows important messages specific to Internet Explorer. These are usually links to other pages or computers. |
| Links | Denotes a hyperlink from the current words or graphic to another page or document. Links are usually indicated by a different color and/or underlined text. |

Toolbar    Menu bar    Title bar    Minimize    Maximize (restore)    Close

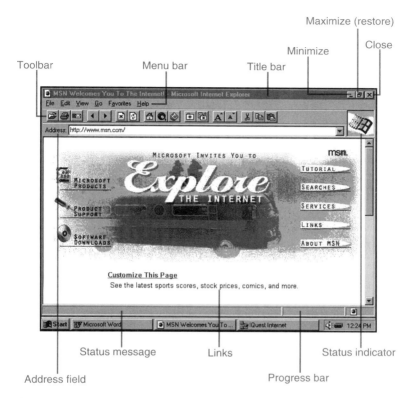

Status message    Links    Status indicator

Address field    Progress bar

**FIGURE 11.2**    Internet Explorer window features.

# USING INTERNET EXPLORER HELP

Unlike Netscape, Internet Explorer provides a help file that can be accessed through the standard Windows 95 Help system.

**TIP**    **Help for Help**    For more information on the Windows 95 Help system, refer to the Windows 95 primer in the back of this book or the *10 Minute Guide to Windows 95*.

Any of the three methods described below will allow you to access help for Internet Explorer.

1. **Contents**   Provides you with general topics that you can select to narrow your search to a specific topic.

2. **Index**   Allows you to type in a topic and access related help index sections.

3. **Find**   Allows you to type in a topic, provides you with a list of related words, and allows you to access related help index sections.

# EXITING MICROSOFT INTERNET EXPLORER

To exit Microsoft Internet Explorer, use one of the following methods:

* On the Menu bar, open the File menu and click Exit.

* Click the Close (X) button in the upper right-hand corner of the window.

In this lesson, you learned how to open and exit Microsoft Internet Explorer. You also learned about the Explorer screen features and Help features. In the next lesson, you will learn how to reset your company's intranet home page and how to use the toolbar.

# NAVIGATING WITH INTERNET EXPLORER

LESSON 12

*In this lesson, you learn how to use the toolbar,
access and set your home page, use links, and use the Open function for
Microsoft's Internet Explorer.*

## USING THE TOOLBAR

The toolbar located at the top of the Internet Explorer toolbar
allows you to navigate quickly through intranet pages (see Figure
12.1).

Toolbar —

**FIGURE 12.1**   The Internet Explorer Browser Toolbar.

Table 12.1 identifies each button on the toolbar and describes
what it does.

TABLE 12.1   TOOLBAR BUTTON FUNCTIONS

| BUTTON | NAME | DESCRIPTION |
|---|---|---|
| ◀ | Back | Takes you back to the previous page displayed. For example, if you click Back three times, Internet Explorer will display the last three pages you viewed. |
| ▶ | Forward | Takes you to the page that was displayed before you clicked the Back button. This button is dependent on whether you have used the Back button. |
| 🏠 | Open Start Page | Displays the default page set up by your system administrator or that you have designated to be displayed first. |
| 🔄 | Refresh | Reloads and displays the current page again. You will only use this button if the page you are viewing has changed since the last time you load it or if there is a problem with the loaded page. |
| ⊞ | Open Favorites | Allows you to enter an intranet address that you have previously set as a Favorite. |

| BUTTON | NAME | DESCRIPTION |
|--------|------|-------------|
| | Open | Allows you to enter an intranet address that you desire to access. |
| | Print | Prints the current page. |
| | Stop | Allows you halt the down-loading process if you are having difficulty loading a particular page or if you de-cide not to wait for the page to download. |
| | Send | Allows you to send e-mail via your intranet by activating Microsoft Exchange. |

**TIP**    **A Home Page by Any Other Name...**  Start page is the term that Microsoft uses to refer to a home page. As you know, the home page is the first Web page that displays when you start your browser.

# ACCESSING THE HOME PAGE

When you start Internet Explorer, the default *home page* that has been set up by your system administrator appears. This could be a company, department, or personal home page. There may be multiple home pages for your organization; however, access to some of these pages may be restricted and a password may be required.

From a home page, you have the ability to access other pages and relevant company information using links. When you pass your mouse pointer over a link, it automatically changes to a hand symbol, as shown in Figure 12.2. Click a link to jump from the current page to connected text on a different page.

 **Links**    A link connects one intranet page to another. Links are identified by colored and/or underlined text or graphics.

Click a link to jump to a different Web page.

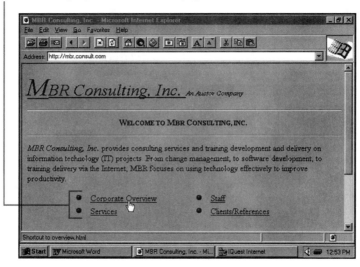

**FIGURE 12.2**    Linked pages.

# RESETTING THE HOME PAGE

After you visit other pages, you may decide to change the home page your system administrator set for you. For example, there may be a particular Web page that you visit daily, that you would like to make your home page so it is the first page you see when you start Internet Explorer.

After you access and display the page that you desire as your home page, proceed with the following steps:

1. In the Menu bar, open the View Menu and click Options. The Options dialog box appears.

2. Click the Start and Search Pages tab to display it, as shown in Figure 12.3.

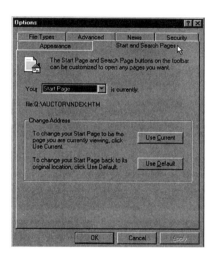

**FIGURE 12.3**   The Start and Search Pages tab.

3. If Start Page is not in the text box labeled "Your [Start Page/Search Page] is currently...", click the down arrow next to the text box and select Start Page, as shown in Figure 12.4.

4. Click the Use Current button, then click OK.

5. When you start Internet Explorer, this page will now be displayed as your home page.

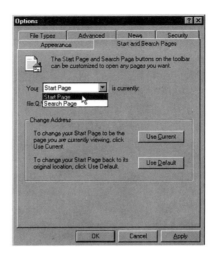

FIGURE 12.4   Select Start Page.

# USING THE HISTORY FOLDER

Suppose you have viewed many pages (five or more) during your current intranet session. Explorer's More History folder provides a speedy alternative for redisplaying a page that you previously accessed.

**A Place in History**   History will store the URL for Web pages you have visited until you choose to delete them or empty the History folder. The folder will hold a maximum of 3000 URLs.

To access Web pages using the History folder, follow these steps:

**1.** Click the File menu. The most recently reviewed pages are listed near the bottom of the menu.

2. If the page you desire is on the list, click that page and it will be displayed again.

3. If you have viewed many pages, the More History option appears at the bottom of the list on the File Menu, as shown in Figure 12.5.

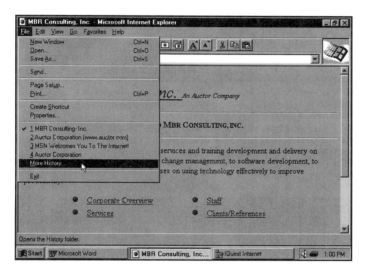

**FIGURE 12.5**    The More History option.

4. If you don't see the page that you desire on the File menu, click the More History option.

5. The Microsoft Internet/History window appears, as shown in Figure 12.6. Double-click the page that you want to display again.

**Figure 12.6**   The Microsoft Internet/History window.

In this lesson, you learned how to access and reset your home page, how to use the toolbar, and how to use the History to navigate in Internet Explorer. In the next lesson, you learn to add, view, and delete Favorite pages in Internet Explorer.

# ADDING, VIEWING, AND DELETING FAVORITES

*In this lesson, you learn how to add, view, and delete favorite intranet pages.*

## ADDING A PAGE TO THE FAVORITES FOLDER

Do you have a favorite story, poem, or anecdote that you read over and over? Chances are you've highlighted or marked this favorite spot with a bookmark so you don't have to search for it every time you want to read it. In Internet Explorer, you can mark your most frequently used or helpful pages on your intranet by creating a Favorites folder. Favorites are like bookmarks—they take you directly to a page without you having to remember how you got there, or the URL for the page.

To add a web page to the Favorites folder, follow these steps:

1. Access a page from your intranet that you use frequently, or that you find helpful.

2. Have this page showing in your browser (see Figure 13.1).

3. Open the Favorites menu, and select Add To Favorites.

4. The Add To Favorites window appears with the highlighted name of the page showing in the Name field (see Figure 13.2). Since the name is highlighted, you can change it to something more meaningful to you by simply typing a new name, if desired.

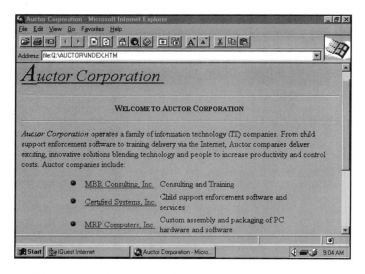

FIGURE 13.1    Favorite page in browser.

FIGURE 13.2    Add button in Add To Favorites window.

**5.** Click the Add button to add this page to your Favorites folder.

**6.** The Add To Favorites window will close, and the page will be added to your Favorites folder.

**Missing in Action**  If you try to access one of your Favorite pages and get an error message, don't worry. The page may have been moved to a new area, deleted, or given a new URL. Lesson 14, "Organizing and Working with Favorites," explains what to do when this occurs.

# VIEWING YOUR FAVORITES

Now that you have added pages to your Favorites folder, follow these steps to view them:

1. Open the Favorites menu.

2. The pages that you have added to the Favorites folder are listed below the Open favorites option, as shown in Figure 13.3.

**FIGURE 13.3**    List of Favorites in Favorites menu.

3. Click one of your Favorites. The page now appears on your browser.

Another way to view your Favorites is to open the Favorites menu, and select the Open Favorites option. The Favorites window appears with icons of the Favorite pages. Double-click one of the icons to have this page appear in browser.

# DELETING FAVORITES

When your Favorites pages are no longer needed, you can take the following steps to delete them from your Favorites folder:

1. Open the Favorites menu and select the Open Favorites option.

2. The Favorites window appears with the Favorites icons.

3. Click the icon of the page you want to delete.

4. Next, click the right mouse button. A drop-down menu appears as shown in Figure 13.4.

**Figure 13.4**    Icon, Drop-down menu, and Delete in Favorites window.

5. Click the Delete command.

6. The Confirm File Delete window appears asking for confirmation of the delete. Click the Yes button to continue, and the No button to cancel the delete.

In this lesson, you learned to add, view, and delete Favorite pages. In the next lesson, you will learn how to organize your Favorites, create subfolders in your Favorites folder, move a document to a subfolder, and change the properties of a Favorites folder entry.

# ORGANIZING AND WORKING WITH FAVORITES

*In this lesson, you learn about creating subfolders, moving Favorites to subfolders, and changing properties of Favorites.*

## CREATING SUBFOLDERS

As you continue to surf your company's intranet you will want to add more Favorites for easy reference. As you know, when you add a Favorite, Internet Explorer simply adds it to your Favorites list. Over time, your Favorites list may become quite lengthy, and you may find it desirable to organize it.

With Internet Explorer you can take your favorite documents and organize them into more than one folder. These other folders are called *subfolders*. You can use any name for your new subfolders. For example, you could have three subfolders named clients, staff, and reports.

To create a subfolder in your Favorites folder follow these steps:

1. Open the Favorites menu and select the Open Favorites option.

2. The Favorites window appears with the Favorites icons displayed. Place your mouse pointer in the window, and click the right mouse button.

3. A drop-down menu appears as shown in Figure 14.1. Select the New option.

**FIGURE 14.1**   The New option in Favorites window.

**4.** A submenu appears as shown in Figure 14.2. Select the Folder option.

**FIGURE 14.2**   Folder options from submenu in Favorites window.

**5.** A new folder is added to the Favorites window with the title **New Folder** highlighted as shown in Figure 14.3.

**6.** Type the title you want for your folder and press the enter key to accept it.

**7.** Close the window by clicking the **Close** (X) button in the upper right corner.

**FIGURE 14.3**    New Folder in Favorites window.

# MOVING A FAVORITE PAGE TO A SUBFOLDER

Once you create a new subfolder, you can move existing pages from the Favorites folder to it. To do this, follow these steps:

1. Open the Favorites menu and select the Open Favorites option. The Favorites window appears with the Favorites icons and any subfolders you created displayed.

2. Drag a page icon to the subfolder you want it in and release the mouse button.

3. Repeat step 2 as many times as necessary.

4. Double-click the subfolder where you have moved a page or pages to open it. A window titled with the name of that subfolder and the icons of the moved pages are displayed.

5. Close both windows by clicking the **Close** (X) button in the upper right corner of each.

## CHANGING FAVORITES PROPERTIES

Sometimes, a page in your Favorites folder or subfolder no longer works. Sometimes the page has been deleted from the server. Usually, however, the page has been moved and its URL is different. You can modify a favorite page to reflect the new location by updating its URL in your Favorites folder. You will have to ask your system administrator or someone else who is responsible for the page what its new address or URL is. Once you have the new address, follow these steps:

1. Open the Favorites menu and select the Open Favorites option.

2. Click the right mouse button on the icon of the page you want to modify.

3. A drop-down menu will appear. Select the Properties option.

4. The Properties window appears. Select the Internet Shortcut tab as shown in Figure 14.4.

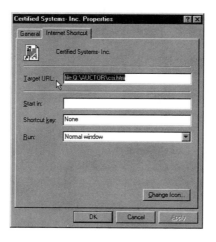

FIGURE 14.4    The Internet Shortcut tab in the Properties window.

5. The Target URL field is highlighted; type in the new URL for the page.

6. Click the OK button to apply the change.

7. The next time you access this page the URL change will be in effect, and the page will appear in your browser.

In this lesson, you learned to organize your Favorite pages by creating subfolders, moving documents into the subfolders, and changing the properties of the favorites. In the next lesson, you will learn how to configure the appearance of your Intranet pages using Internet Explorer.

## LESSON 15

# CONFIGURING EXPLORER'S APPEARANCE

*In this lesson, you learn how to change the look and feel of your Intranet pages by changing the color, fonts, pictures, sounds, animations, and shortcut options in Internet Explorer.*

## CHANGING COLORS

After exploring your company's intranet, you may want to change the appearance of the pages to better suit your needs. One way to do this is to change the colors of the text and backgrounds on the pages.

To change the text and background colors, follow these steps:

1. Open the View menu and select Options. The Appearance tab will be displayed (see Figure 15.1).

2. Under the Page section, click the box beside Use custom colors.

3. Next, click either the Text or the Background button to customize the colors for that particular item.

4. A color palette will appear (see Figure 15.2).

5. Click the desired color square within the color palette.

6. Click the OK button to close the palette.

 **How Will I Know?** If you want to know how colors will appear on your screen, click Apply. This will display your choice and leave the Options window open for further changes.

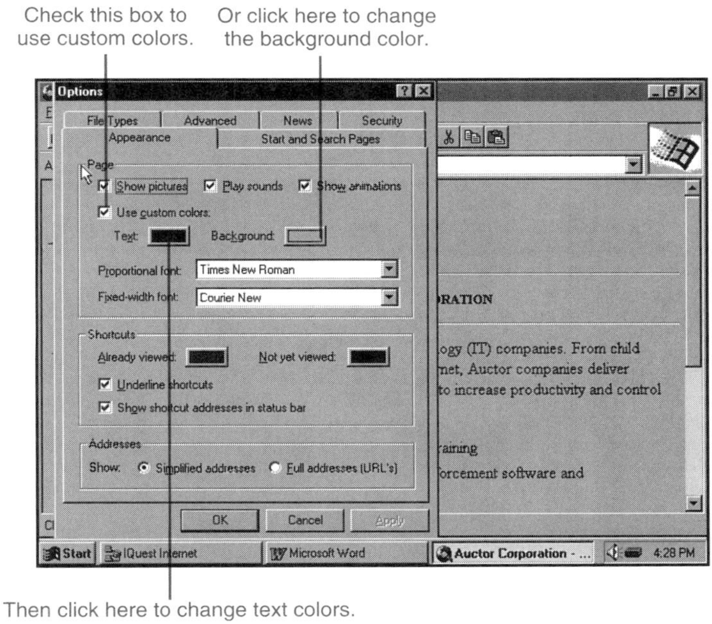

Check this box to    Or click here to change
use custom colors.    the background color.

Then click here to change text colors.

**FIGURE 15.1**    The Appearance tab of the Options dialog box.

**FIGURE 15.2**    The color palette.

**7.** Click Apply to view your changes without closing the
    Options window.

**8.** When you are satisfied with your colors, click the OK button to save the changes, close the Options window, and display the changes in the current Web page.

 **Color Me Crazy**   A Web page may not display the background color that you have selected. If a particular background has been written into the Web page, Internet Explorer will display that background and ignore your choice.

# CHANGING FONT STYLE

In addition to changing the colors of the text and background, you can change the font style that is used when a page appears on your browser.

 **Font**   Font describes the style and size of the text that is displayed on your Web pages. Many different sizes and styles are available to be displayed on your intranet.

**1.** Open the View menu and select Options.

**2.** When the Options window appears, click the Appearance tab.

**3.** Under the Page section, click the down arrow beside either the Proportional font or the Fixed-width font option.

 **Proportional and Fixed-Width**   With proportional fonts, letters occupy space based on their shape. For example, "m" would be wider than "l." With fixed-width fonts, letters are the same width regardless of their shape.

**4.** A drop-down menu appears listing the different font styles (see Figure 15.3).

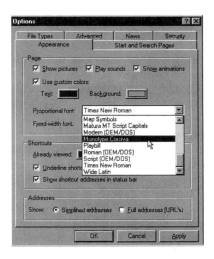

**Figure 15.3** Selecting a font style from the drop-down list.

**5.** Click the desired style.

**6.** Click the OK button on the Options window to apply the new font style.

**Why Didn't It Work?** Some pages and documents may have a preselected font style embedded in the HTML coding, and therefore when accessed, will not display the font style you have chosen.

# Changing Font Size

You can also change the size of the font you view on the pages for easier readability.

**1.** Open the View menu and select Fonts.

2. Select the desired font size from the pop-up submenu that appears (see Figure 15.4).

**Figure 15.4**    Choosing a relative font size from the Fonts submenu.

3. Once you choose a new size, it will immediately be applied to the document you are now viewing.

  **A Quick Change**    Another way to change the font size is to click the Use Larger Font or Use Smaller Font button on the toolbar. Clicking these buttons will immediately change the font size in the document you are now viewing.

# Changing Pictures, Sounds, or Animations Settings

Occasionally, you will want to view only the text of a document and not its corresponding graphics, sounds, or animations. Changing some or all of these options will cause pages to load more quickly.

To disable graphics, sounds, or animations, follow these steps:

1. Open the View menu and select Options.

2. When the Options window appears, click the Appearance tab.

**3.** Within the Page section, click any or all of the following options to remove the check mark: **Show pictures**, **Play sounds**, or **Show animations** (see Figure 15.5).

The picture, sound, and animations options

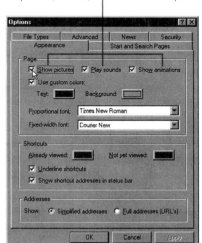

**FIGURE 15.5**    Unchecking options.

**4.** After removing the check marks, click the OK button on the Options window to apply the changes.

# CHANGING SHORTCUT APPEARANCES

Shortcuts are Internet Explorer's equivalent to links. They appear as text or graphics that are highlighted, underlined, or both. When clicked, shortcuts take you directly to the Intranet page "linked" to that shortcut. You will know when you encounter a shortcut because the mouse pointer will change to a hand with a pointing finger when it moves over a shortcut.

Normally, your system will display the default color values, determine whether the shortcuts should be underlined and show the addresses in the Status Bar field. You can, however, modify these options with the following steps:

1. Open the View menu and select Options.

2. Within the Shortcuts section of the Options dialog box, click the color boxes next to **Already viewed** and/or **Not yet viewed**, to change the color of your shortcuts (see Figure 15.6).

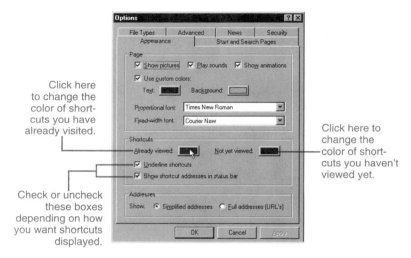

Click here to change the color of short-cuts you have already visited.

Click here to change the color of short-cuts you haven't viewed yet.

Check or uncheck these boxes depending on how you want shortcuts displayed.

**Figure 15.6**   Changing shortcut options.

3. A color palette appears.

4. Click a color square within the palette.

5. Click the OK button to close the palette.

6. Click the Underline shortcuts or Show shortcut addresses in status bar boxes to remove the check marks.

7. Removing the check marks for these options causes the shortcuts not to be underlined, or have their URLs appear in the Status Bar.

8. Click Apply to view your changes without closing the Options window.

**9.** When you are satisfied with your choices, click OK to save the changes, close the Options window, and display the changes in the current Web page.

In this lesson, you learned how to change the appearance of your intranet pages. In the next lesson, you will learn how to configure Internet Explorer's advanced preferences.

# LESSON 16

# CONFIGURING EXPLORER'S ADVANCED OPTIONS

*In this lesson, you learn to configure Internet Explorer's Document Cache Options and how to use the History feature.*

## CONFIGURING THE DOCUMENT CACHE OPTIONS

When you visit a Web page on your intranet the first time, you may notice that it takes some time for it to completely display. Then, when you revisit that page, it seems to display almost instantaneously. This is due to a feature known as *cache*. The document cache remembers web pages that you have accessed and stores them locally on your PC. This feature eliminates the time it takes to reload a page from the network. Rather than loading the network version each time you visit a page, Internet Explorer may load it from your cache. There are several settings that allow you to control the use of cache on your PC.

 **Cache** A *cache* or *document cache* is a storage area for web pages that you have accessed on your intranet.

## CHANGING THE UPDATE PAGES DEFAULT

You have two options for controlling the frequency of retrieving information over the network.

**Update pages once per session**    Selecting this option tells Internet Explorer that you want to view the most current version of an intranet page. In this case, the network version of a page will always be retrieved the first time it is visited during any session on your intranet. Subsequent visits to that page in the same session will use the cached version. This is the default setting.

**Update pages never**    Selecting this option tells Internet Explorer to always retrieve a desired page from your cache if it is available. In this case, Internet Explorer will not automatically update to the most current version from the network.

**TIP**

**Never Say Never**    Although the "Update pages never" option will not load the most current intranet information automatically, a page can always be updated by using the Refresh button. Clicking the Refresh button will retrieve and display the network version of a page.

"Update pages once per session" will give you the most current version of a page the first time you visit it in a session; however, using "Update pages never" will display the information more quickly. To configure Internet Explorer so that it doesn't automatically retrieve the network version of a document, follow these steps:

1.  Open the View menu and select the Options command. You will see the Options window.

2.  Click the Advanced tab at the top of the window.

3.  Within the Cache section, click the button beside the Never option (see Figure 16.1).

4.  Click the OK button in the Options window to save the change and return to the current web page.

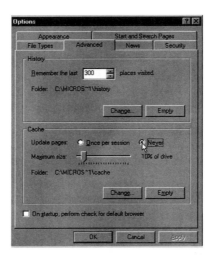

**FIGURE 16.1**    Clicking the Never option.

**To Change or Not to Change?**    Most corporate networks have the power and capacity to transmit information quickly; therefore, you probably will not need to change your default settings unless you use a slower connection such as remote or dial-up access (see Lesson 3).

## CHANGING THE SIZE OF THE DOCUMENT CACHE

By default, Internet Explorer uses a maximum of 10 percent of your total hard disk space to store pages and graphics. If you want to change this to use more or less disk space, you can specify the percentage. For example, if you have a large hard drive capacity, you may want to use less than 10 percent. On the other hand, your system administrator may request that you have a large cache to limit network traffic.

To change the size of the document cache, follow these steps:

1. Open the View menu and select Options.

2. When the Options window appears, click the Advanced tab.

3. Within the Cache section, move the slider next to the Maximum size option to a desired percentage (see Figure 16.2).

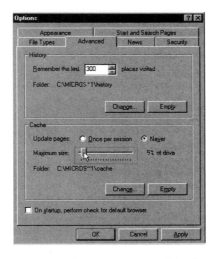

**Figure 16.2**   Moving the Cache section slider bar.

4. Click the Apply button to apply the change without closing the Options window.

5. Make any other changes and click the OK button in the Options window to close the window, save your changes, and return to the current web page.

## CHANGING THE LOCATION OF THE DOCUMENT CACHE

By default, Internet Explorer will place the document Cache in a folder on your hard drive. You can change this location by following these steps:

1. Open the View menu and select Options.

2. When the Options window appears, click the Advanced tab.

3. In the Cache area, make a note of the current location of the Cache. This is listed next to the word **Folder**.

4. Click the Change button (see Figure 16.3).

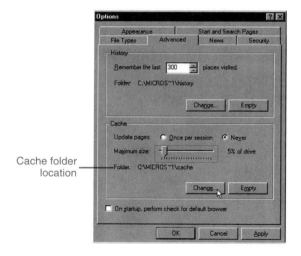

Cache folder location

**FIGURE 16.3**    Changing the cache location.

5. The Browse for Folder window displays (see Figure 16.4).

6. Click the location where you would like your Cache folder saved.

**7.** Click the OK button to close this window.

**8.** Click the OK button in the Options window to apply the changes.

**FIGURE 16.4**    The Browse for Folder window.

## EMPTYING THE DOCUMENT CACHE

If your cached documents are taking up too much room on your hard drive, you can delete all the information and start over.

To empty your document cache, follow these steps:

**1.** Open the View menu and select Options.

**2.** When the Options window appears, click the Advanced tab.

**3.** Within the Cache section, click the Empty button.

**4.** You are asked to confirm whether you want to empty the cache (see Figure 16.5). Click Yes to empty the Disk Cache folder now; click No to cancel this action.

**5.** Click the OK button to close the Options window.

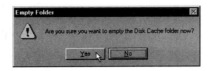

**Figure 16.5**   You're given a chance to change your mind.

# Changing the History Options

In life, history is kept to record prominent events. Internet Explorer uses the History feature to keep a list of previously visited intranet pages so that you can easily locate pages that are of interest to you.

Setting the History option allows you to modify the number of previously viewed pages that Explorer remembers and displays, change the location of where the names and addresses of these pages are stored on your hard disk, and empty the history folder.

## Changing the Number of Pages Remembered in the History Folder

Internet Explorer has a set default value for the number of pages your history folder will store. To change this number, follow these steps:

1. Open the View menu and select Options.

2. When the Options window displays, click the Advanced tab.

3. Within the History section, type the number of documents you want to have remembered in the text box within the **Remember the last...places visited** option.

**TIP**   **Pointing the Way**   You can also click the arrows beside the text box and numerical values will be increased or decreased accordingly. These buttons work just like your TV remote control.

**4.** Click the Apply button to apply the change without closing the Options window.

**5.** Make any other changes and click the OK button in the Options window to close the window, save your changes and return to the current web page.

## CHANGING WHERE PAGE NAMES AND ADDRESSES ARE STORED

**1.** Open the View menu and select Options.

**2.** When the Options window displays, click the Advanced tab.

**3.** Within the History section, click the Change button.

**4.** The Browse for Folder window appears.

**5.** Click the new location where you would like your History folder with the stored sites to reside (see Figure 16.6).

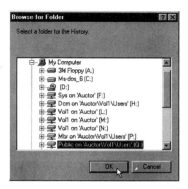

**FIGURE 16.6**   A new location selected in the Browse for Folder window.

6. Click the OK button to close the Browse for Folder window.

7. When you have completed your changes, click the OK button to close the Options window and return to the current web page.

## Emptying Your History Folder

If your History folder becomes too large to manage, you can empty it and start a new list. To do so, follow these steps:

1. Open the View menu and select Options.

2. When the Options window displays, click the Advanced tab.

3. Within the History section, click the Empty button.

4. You are asked whether you are sure you want to empty the folder.

5. Click the Yes button to empty your History folder, or click No to cancel this operation.

6. When you have completed your changes, click the OK button to close the Options window.

In this lesson, you learned how to configure the advanced and technical options of Internet Explorer. In the next lesson, you will learn how to use Internet Explorer's E-mail feature.

# USING INTERNET EXPLORER E-MAIL

*In this lesson, you learn how to send e-mail messages and accompanying documents using Microsoft's Internet Explorer.*

## WHAT IS E-MAIL?

*E-mail* is short for electronic mail. Basically, it is information addressed and transmitted over networks. Compared to regular mail, e-mail is very fast. There are many types of software for e-mail. The Internet Explorer browser includes an easy-to-use e-mail capability.

In its simplest form, all e-mail has three parts:

1. The recipient's address, such as **mbr@auctor.com**

2. The subject line

3. The content of the message

## WHAT IS YOUR INTRANET ADDRESS?

Obviously, to send or receive e-mail, you must have an *address*. Persons who use the Internet to send e-mail probably know a recipient's address is usually the recipient's name or initials plus the Internet site separated by the @ sign. E-mail in Explorer via an intranet usually involves using the recipient's log-in name for the address. However, this configuration depends on how your mail administrator sets it up.

**Who Are You?**   If you do not know your e-mail address, contact your mail administrator. This person may be different from your system administrator.

# Sending a Simple E-Mail Message

Sending messages via e-mail is a quick and convenient way to relay information. Although you cannot currently receive mail through Microsoft's Internet Explorer, you can send it.

**Special Delivery**   Microsoft Exchange is the Windows 95 e-mail application and is not a part of Internet Explorer. The only Microsoft Exchange function that you can access from Internet Explorer is the New Message function. If you would like more information regarding Microsoft Exchange, please contact your mail administrator.

**No E-Mail?**   Your mail administrator should already have configured Microsoft Exchange. If Internet Explorer's e-mail does not function properly—you are unable to send e-mail, or no one receives e-mail you send—contact your mail administrator.

Use the following steps to send e-mail through Microsoft's Internet Explorer:

1. From the Microsoft Internet Explorer window, click the envelope icon located on the Toolbar or open the File menu and click Send.

**Let Me In!**   When you access e-mail from Internet Explorer, you may be required to choose a profile, such as "Internet Mail Settings," and enter a password.

**2.** The New Message-Microsoft Exchange window displays, as shown in Figure 17.1.

Send mail button        Insert file button

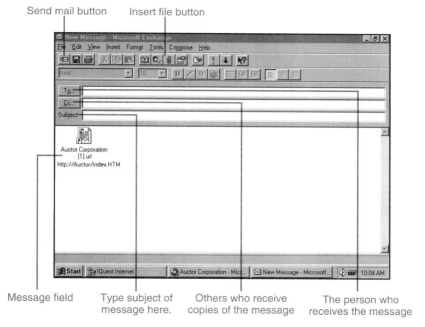

Message field        Type subject of        Others who receive        The person who
                     message here.        copies of the message    receives the message

**FIGURE 17.1**    The New Message-Microsoft Exchange window.

**3.** Type the recipient's e-mail address in the To... field.

**4.** Press the Tab key to advance to the Cc... field. If another individual needs to receive a copy of the message, type his or her e-mail address in the Cc... field to be carbon copied.

**5.** Press the Tab key to advance to the Subject: field. Type the subject of your message if you desire.

6. Press the Tab key to advance to the message area. By default, Microsoft's Internet Explorer includes the intranet page you are currently viewing as an attachment at the beginning of your message.

7. If you do not wish to send the URL attachment, select URL information and press the Delete key on your keyboard.

8. Type the message you want to send.

9. Click the Send Message button on the toolbar or open the File menu and click Send to send the message.

10. The message is sent to the mail server and routed to the recipient and the New Message-Microsoft Exchange window closes.

**For Your Eyes Only?**   Be aware that someone like the system or mail administrator can always read what is in mailboxes. The Electronic Privacy Act of 1986 provides some privacy guidelines; however, if you are writing something during regular work hours, the Act may not protect you from actions taken if you send something inappropriate in an e-mail message.

## INSERTING FILES

When sending e-mail, you may find it desirable to send accompanying documents created in other software applications such as Word. These extra documents are known as *inserted files*, and sending these documents through Explorer e-mail is described as *inserting files*.

**Inserted Files**   Inserted files are computer files that accompany the message portion of your e-mail. For example, an e-mail message might be "Fred, I'm sending you the April sales report." An inserted file might be a spreadsheet file containing the actual sales statistics.

When you insert a file into your e-mail message, keep in mind that the recipient must have the same application in which the file was created in order to view or change it. If the recipient does not have the same software, the inserted file must be converted to another format. For example, if you send an inserted file that is a Microsoft Excel file and the recipient does not have Microsoft Excel on the receiving PC, the recipient is unable to use the Excel file, even though he or she receives and can read the e-mail message accompanying the Excel file.

From the New Message-Microsoft Exchange window, there is a simple method for accessing the documents (files) you desire to insert. To insert a file, use the following steps:

1. From the New Message-Microsoft Exchange window, click the Insert button located on the toolbar or open the Insert menu and click File. The Insert File dialog box appears, as shown in Figure 17.2.

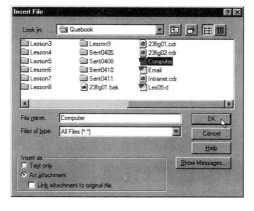

FIGURE 17.2   The Insert File dialog box.

2. Choose the file you wish to insert and click OK.

3. The file displays as an icon in the message area of the New Message-Microsoft Exchange window, as shown in Figure 17.3.

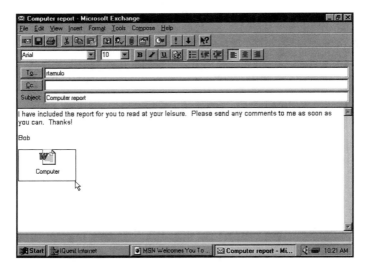

FIGURE 17.3    A file icon in the message area.

In this lesson, you learned how to send e-mail messages and accompanying documents with Explorer. In the next lesson, you will learn how to find information on a large intranet.

# FINDING INFORMATION ON A LARGE INTRANET

*In this lesson, you learn one way, other than point and click naviga-
tion, to find information on some intranets.*

## WHAT HAPPENS WHEN AN INTRANET GROWS?

To this point, we have been discussing fairly simple information
presented on an intranet. Simple, well-organized intranet pages
and links allow users to start at the home page, link to a topic,
and quickly navigate to more detailed or related pages of information. Navigating in this manner is all you need to do in many
situations.

However, as an intranet grows and more departments add content, finding information can become more troublesome or time-
consuming. In addition, as more users gain access to the intranet,
it becomes increasingly difficult to define and connect links that
will allow any employee from any department to navigate quickly
and easily to the information that employee seeks.

Some organizations are addressing this problem by setting up
several home pages. Individual departments could each have a
home page with links to relevant departmental information. The
approach at least provides logical starting points for a user to find
information through links.

Other organizations are taking the approach of cataloging information into hierarchical lists by subject area. For example, a user
looking for information on sick leave might begin by clicking the

Human Resources Department from a subject list of all departments in the company. That would lead to a page containing Human Resource topics including policies. Clicking policies would lead to a page containing sick leave policy, which would then link to the page containing the desired information.

Alternatively, some organizations are making search engines available to users to assist in finding information that cannot be linked to readily.

# WHAT ARE SEARCH ENGINES?

**Search Engines**   Software programs that search intranet pages for words, phrases, or concepts typed by a user. When matches are found, the addresses of the pages containing the matches are displayed, and the user can follow a link directly to any page containing a match.

*Search engine* is a term that applies to tools for finding information on an intranet. There are really two separate capabilities of a search engine.

The first component is a data gathering and indexing function. This function looks at the pages on an intranet, builds a database of information about these pages, and cross-references the database entries to the pages' locations (URLs). When building the database, some search engines look only at the page title, some look at the first paragraph on a page, and others look at and index every word on a page.

The second component is the part of the search engine that compares the words or phrases that you are looking for with the information collected and indexed by the first component. This component varies in sophistication from using simple word match logic to using complex statistical algorithms and fuzzy logic. This searching/matching component is what is generally referred to as a search engine.

Many search engines are available today, but not all intranets have such a capability. Some search engines are free; others are expensive. Requirements and uses also vary widely.

# COMMON SEARCH ENGINE FEATURES

There are certain capabilities common to most search engines, although they may be implemented quite differently. These capabilities include the following:

**Forms Input**    You will have the ability to type your search words or phrases into a blank field on a form. Most then contain a button to execute the search (**Submit**, **Search**, and **Find** are common labels).

**Boolean Logic**    Most allow you to narrow your search by specifying the requirement to match combinations (one term **and** another, one term **or** another).

**Proximity Searches**    You can specify that terms be located within a certain number of words of each other, thus increasing the probability that they refer to the same topic.

**Wild Cards**    This capability allows pattern-matching searching. If **\*** is a wild card, the searching for **stor\*** will find examples of **store**, **storm**, and so forth.

**Inclusion**    You can specify specific terms to be included or excluded from a match. These are usually preceded with + for inclusion and – for exclusion. See the example in the next section for refining a search with the inclusion capability.

**Relevancy Ranking**    Almost all search engines attempt to convey what they think are the best results based on your inquiry. Some list the results in priority order. Others assign a numeric score to judge what is best, say 100 down to 1. Others make suggestions for similar pages to look at. Still others display a portion of the page along with the link.

**You Be the Judge**　No matter what search engine you use, always scroll through the results and use your judgment about relevancy. Ranking is more of an art than a science in some cases.

# How to Use a Search Engine—
# An Example from the Internet

As mentioned previously, although different search engines may be designed differently, in general, you use all search engines by performing similar steps. The following is an example using the Alta Vista search engine from Digital Equipment Corporation with the inclusion feature.

 **Start Your Engines!**　If your intranet has a search capability, note that it may be packaged, configured, and presented in any number of ways, and therefore, may look very different from the example in this lesson.

1. Type the words or phrases about which you want to find information into the box to the left of the Submit button. In this example we are using **vacations** (see Figure 18.1).

2. Press Enter or click the Submit button to start the search.

3. View the links displayed by the search engine to the pages that contain the word **vacations**. Note that there are far more matches than you'd ever want to search (see Figure 18.2).

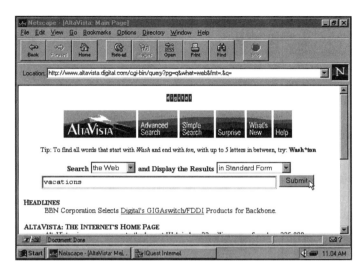

FIGURE 18.1     Beginning the Alta Vista search.

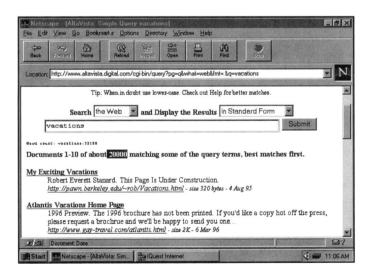

FIGURE 18.2     "vacations" matches.

**4.** Click the address of any page returned by the search engine to visit and read the information therein.

**5.** Use the back and forward buttons on the toolbar to explore as many of the pages returned by the search engine as desired.

**6.** Refine the search by adding **+Hawaii** to **vacations** and click Submit.

**7.** View the links displayed by the search engine to the pages that contain the words **vacations** and **Hawaii**. Note that there are now 97 matches (see Figure 18.3).

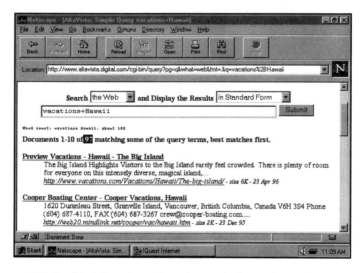

**FIGURE 18.3** Matches for refined search "vacations+Hawaii."

**8.** Refine the search by adding **+golf** to **vacations+Hawaii** and click Submit.

**9.** View the links displayed by the search engine to the pages that contain the words **vacations**, **Hawaii**, and **golf**. Note that there is only one match. (See Figure 18.4.)

**10.** Use bookmarks or favorites to capture the addresses of any pages you might want to remember for future visits.

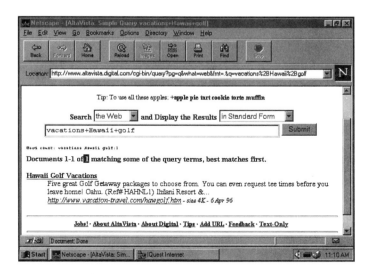

**FIGURE 18.4**    Final results of "vacations+Hawaii+golf."

 **TIP**

**Less Is More**    Lots of matches mean lots of work. The more specific you can be, the more relevant your results will be.

This example has illustrated how one of the features, inclusion, of a typical search engine can help to narrow a search. If you have access to a search engine, the best way to learn about its features, functions, strengths, and weaknesses is to try it out and experiment with its capabilities. Don't forget that most have valuable tips and examples in their Help functions.

**No Matches?**    Don't worry. Try alternative ways to describe what you're seeking, such as synonyms or different ways of phrasing your search. In one sense, search engines can be obtuse. You'll probably find something that works; however, the information you are looking for simply may not be on your intranet.

## SOME POPULAR SEARCH ENGINES YOU MAY ENCOUNTER

Some of the commercial Internet search engines that you may find in some form on your company's intranet now or in the future are as follows:

- Alta Vista, used in the example above, is fast and comprehensive. It searches the full-text of Web pages and is appropriate for beginners. It also has many advanced search features. Users can search for exact matches, include or exclude words, and use wild cards and Boolean logic (and, or, not, near). The first few words of the lead paragraph plus the links are presented as search results.

- Excite offers a friendly, customizable user interface and allows searching by key words and also by concept. With concept search, Excite attempts to find "what you mean" not just "what you say." Excite returns a document summary, the link to the document and a percentage ranking (1–100) indicating its assessment of how well the document matches your query. (100% is a good match.)

- Infoseek Guide has an interesting and easy-to-use interface. Users can search by both key words and phrases. Putting a phrase in double quotes ("") tells Infoseek to find an exact match on the phrase. Putting a hyphen between words indicates that you are looking for the words to be within one word of each other. Infoseek also provides a hierarchical subject list of reviewed pages for browsing and dulling down through links to find information. Infoseek returns the first few sentences of a document, its score (1–100, 100 being the best match), its link, a link to similar pages, and a list of related topics.

- Lycos is one of the first search engines, originally developed by Carnegie Mellon University. It is undergoing rapid change promising many expanded capabilities over the original. Users can perform simple Boolean key word searches and ask for matches to be "stronger" or "looser" to control the number of documents matched and re-turned. Lycos also provides a category list of topics where one can use a combination drill down and search technique to find information. Advanced search capabilities are available by selecting an "Enhance Your Search" option. Lycos returns an ordered list of match pages, each page's score (0–1, 1 being the best match), its link, and an abstract of the page.

- Open Text Index is one of the most sophisticated search engines. This search entry form is easy to use with drop-down selection boxes for setting search parameters. Users can enter words or phrases, connect them with a wide variety of Boolean operators (and, or, but not, near, followed by) and specify where the words are to be found (anywhere, summary, title, first heading, URL). Open Text returns an ordered list of matched pages (best matches first), each page's link, an option to view the matches on the page, and an option to find similar pages.

In this lesson, you learned how to find information in a large intranet using a search engine. In the next lesson, you learn about interactive intranet pages.

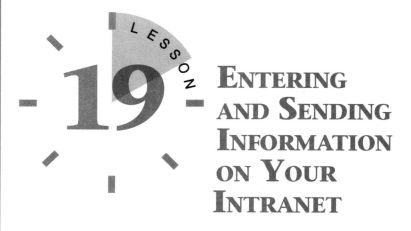

# LESSON 19

# ENTERING AND SENDING INFORMATION ON YOUR INTRANET

*In this lesson, you learn various methods for entering and sending data on your intranet.*

## ENTERING INFORMATION

So far, you have learned about an intranet as a static medium—a technology for passive viewing of information. Intranet browsers typically provide an additional capability for user interaction. This means that you, the reader, can enter, supply, or submit data requested on an intranet page designed as a form.

In most companies, paper is still the most popular medium for information exchange. Memos, surveys, and questionnaires are typed, copied, completed, stored, and retyped ad infinitum. This paper trail is inefficient, expensive, and time consuming.

Intranet technology can address these shortcomings and increase productivity throughout an organization. Intranet forms are used for everything from insurance to personnel to training. Pages within your intranet may contain areas where you can respond to a question by typing information in a box, clicking radio buttons, or selecting an item from a drop-down menu box. Once entered, this information can be sent to some other intranet address either by using e-mail or clicking a "submit" button. In these ways, data collection is centralized, simplified, and made more timely.

Following are some examples of data entry methods being used on intranets. If data collection is part of your intranet, it may be designed and presented differently. However, you would probably follow similar steps. The examples below are for illustration only.

## TEXT BOXES

Text boxes are blank areas where you enter either required information, or free-form text as illustrated in Figure 19.1:

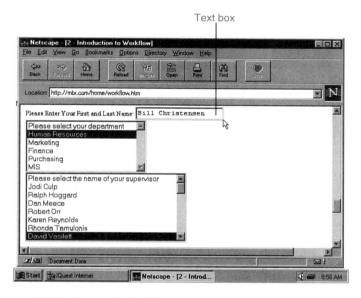

FIGURE 19.1    A sample text box.

Entering data in a text box requires that you type the information in the blank box. Generally, your cursor will be blinking at the beginning of the box. If not, click the mouse pointer in the box to begin typing.

## Option Buttons

Option buttons are similar to the row of push buttons that used to be found on all automobile radios for station selection. Option buttons allow you to choose *one* selection at a time from a list of many (push the button). Clicking the button beside the desired choice causes that button to be highlighted and your choice to be selected. Figure 19.2 illustrates the use of radio buttons to give a multipoint test. If you change your mind, you simply click another button.

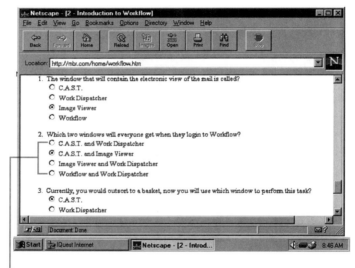

Option buttons

**Figure 19.2**    Sample radio buttons.

## Check Boxes

Check boxes are a variation of option buttons. Instead of clicking a button to make a selection, you click a blank box beside the desired choice. As illustrated in Figure 19.3, a check mark will appear to mark your choice. With check boxes, you can select as many options as you like.

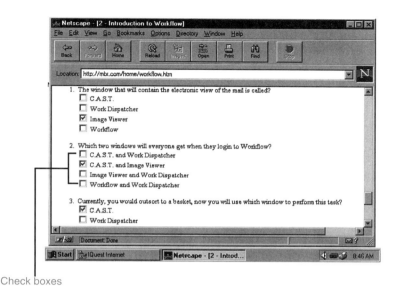

Check boxes

**FIGURE 19.3** Sample check boxes.

## DROP-DOWN BOXES

When you have a long list of items to select from, they may appear awkward when viewed as a list on your browser. To organize this type of list, drop-down boxes are often used. These boxes show only a few items at a time, and let you scroll up or down through the list to view the remaining items. To select an item from anywhere in the list, simply click it (see Figure 19.4).

**Drop-Down Boxes** Drop-down boxes are boxes that appear with choices for you to select. You may have heard them referred to as lists, select elements, or pop-up lists.

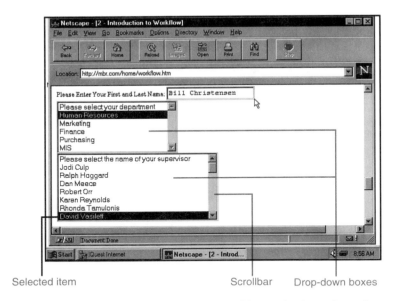

Selected item                    Scrollbar    Drop-down boxes

**FIGURE 19.4**    Scrollbars and selected items in drop-down boxes.

# SENDING INFORMATION

Once you have entered the required information on a page using one or several of the above methods, you can send this information to the proper department or person. Two of the most commonly used methods are e-mail and the *submit* button. Below are examples of how they might operate.

## E-MAIL

In Lessons 10 and 17, you learned how to use intranet e-mail. Some Web pages that you encounter allow you to click a link or shortcut that causes an e-mail window to appear. When the window appears, enter the data in the message area and click send, as shown in Figure 19.5.

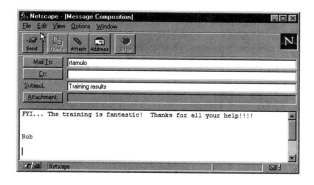

**FIGURE 19.5**    Sample e-mail drop-down window.

## SUBMIT BUTTON

Another method of sending interactive responses is to click a Submit button. At the bottom of many forms is a button that, when clicked, will send the information on its way. The button may or may not be labeled submit. In Figure 19.6, the submit button is labeled **How Did I Do?**; clicking the button submits the answers to a multi-choice test (in other words, sends the answers to one or more intranet addresses).

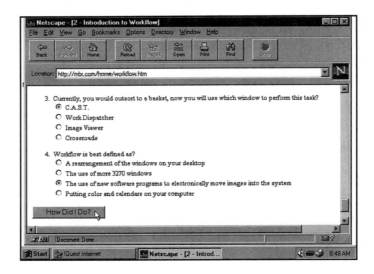

**FIGURE 19.6**   Submit button: "How Did I Do?"

In this lesson, you learned various ways to enter and send information on interactive intranet forms. In the next lesson, you will learn about training via an intranet.

# TRAINING VIA AN INTRANET

*In this lesson, you learn how an intranet can be used to train employees.*

## WHY TRAIN VIA AN INTRANET?

One of the most exciting uses for intranet technology is the delivery of training. Do you remember when you had to leave your desk, and perhaps your office, to go to a classroom to learn material, most of which you forgot by the time you got back? Do you remember the frustration of not being able to move on when you felt comfortable with the material because someone else didn't?

An intranet training course is tailor-made to address these and other shortcomings in traditional training. Students receive material at their desks; learning is self-paced; everyone moves at their own speed. The material can always be available at the desktop for future reference and performance support. And because multimedia technology (sound and video) is available on intranets, materials can be presented in interesting and stimulating formats.

In this lesson, you see examples of two types of training approaches:

- Short packets of information to be used immediately

- A lesson series with comprehension testing

If training is delivered on your intranet, it may be designed and presented differently from these examples. However, you would probably follow similar steps. The examples that follow are for illustration only. You should read each step and look at the referenced figure to understand the concepts and how these types of training could be delivered.

# EXAMPLE 1: "TIP OF THE DAY"

This example involves the delivery of very short snippets of information intended to be put to use immediately. This type of training is typically packaged and presented as a **Tip A Day**, **What's New**, **Clue of the Day**, or **Did You Know That...** button or icon on your opening intranet page, as shown in Figure 20.1.

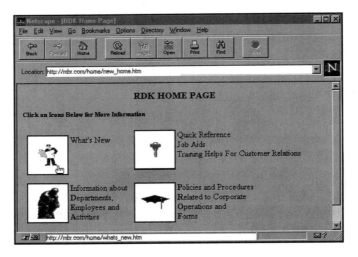

**FIGURE 20.1**    Intranet opening screen.

Figure 20.1 depicts the opening screen from a sample intranet. To help train its employees how to use their computer systems more efficiently, this company publishes a daily time-savings tip, the **Tip of the Day**. The steps you would follow on this intranet to access the daily tip are:

**1.** Click the What's New icon on the page in the upper-left quarter of the screen. This takes you to the **What's New** page (see Figure 20.2).

**2.** On this page, click Tip of the Day, which links you to the current day's tip (see Figure 20.3).

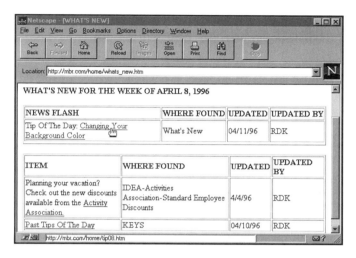

**FIGURE 20.2**    What's New and links.

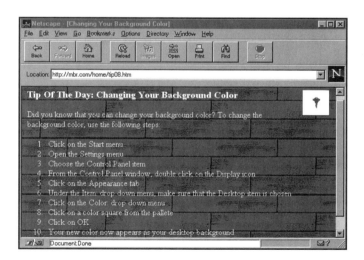

**FIGURE 20.3**    Tip of the Day.

**3.** Click the Back button on the toolbar to return to the previous page (refer to Figure 20.2). Note that on the

**What's New** page (refer to Figure 20.2), there is a link called **Past Tips of the Day**. Clicking this link would take you to a list of prior **Tips of the Day**.

4. Clicking any of these links takes you to the corresponding material for the tip selected.

5. Repeat steps 3 and 4 to review as many tips as you want.

 **TIP**    **Homeward Bound**    At any time, you can click repeatedly on the Back button to return to your intranet's home page. Or you can click the Home button in Netscape or the Start Page button in Internet Explorer and return to your home page immediately.

## EXAMPLE 2: LESSON SERIES WITH COMPREHENSION TESTING

This example (see Figure 20.4) involves a more extensive presentation of material. A series of lessons teaches a company's customer service agents how to use an imaging/workflow system that electronically delivers scanned copies of customer correspondence to an agent's computer. The lessons are designed to be read in approximately 15 minutes, with comprehension testing upon completion.

Figure 20.4 depicts the table of lessons page from the sample intranet. If you were a customer service agent receiving training on this company's intranet, you would take the following steps:

1. Click Lesson 2 to go to the lesson entitled **Introduction to Workflow**. This takes you to the beginning of the lesson (see Figure 20.5).

2. Use the scroll bar on the right side of the screen to move up and down through the material and read the lesson.

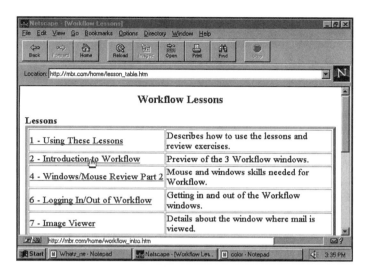

**FIGURE 20.4**     Sample intranet lessons page.

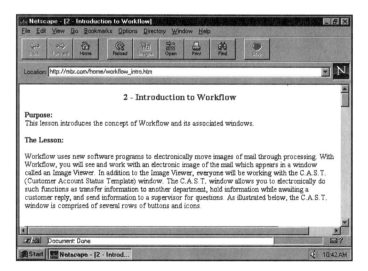

**FIGURE 20.5**     A lesson beginning.

**3.** When finished, scroll to the bottom of the page and click the Review Exercises button (see Figure 20.6).

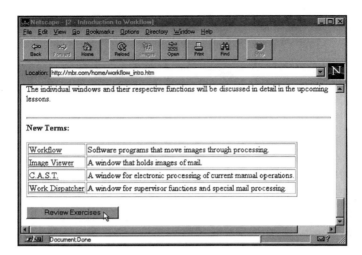

FIGURE 20.6    The Review Exercises button.

**4.** The Review Exercises button links to a series of questions to test your comprehension of the material in the lesson (see Figure 20.7).

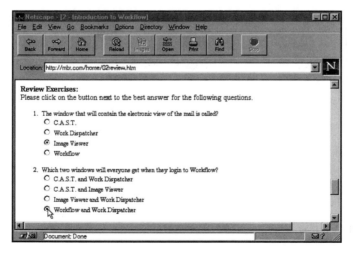

FIGURE 20.7    Comprehension questions.

**5.** Answer each question by clicking the button beside what you think is the correct option (refer to Figure 20.7).

**6.** When finished with all questions, click the How Did I Do? button at the bottom (see Figure 20.8).

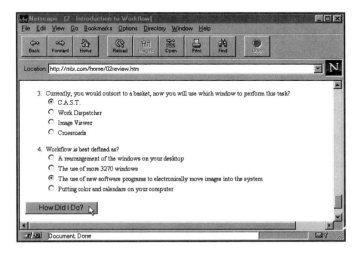

**FIGURE 20.8**  "How Did I Do?"—exercise submission.

**7.** You are linked to a page where your answers are evaluated and scored (see Figure 20.9).

**8.** Click the Back button on the toolbar as many times as required to return you to the table of lessons.

**9.** Repeat steps 1 through 8 to take other lessons in the table.

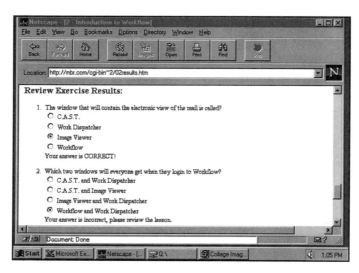

**FIGURE 20.9**    Answer scoring.

In this lesson, you learned about training delivery on the intranet. In the next lesson, you learn about directions intranets are moving and some exciting new products and concepts.

# EMERGING CAPABILITIES FOR INTRANETS

*In this lesson you will learn about some of the latest Internet technology which will probably make its way to your intranet now or in the near future. You are introduced to Java, VRML, and groupware.*

## DAZZLING DEVELOPMENTS

The speed at which new capabilities and features are being added to the Internet community is mind-boggling and difficult to stay on top of. Some of the products are somewhat esoteric or have limited current applicability. Others offer functionality that is of obvious interest and benefit to corporations using intranets.

The following sections provide an overview of topics which appear at this time to be the ones most likely to be adopted for widespread corporate usage. There are really no buttons to click in this lesson. Just sit back and put on your thinking cap, read the material, and understand the excitement in what's coming now and soon.

## UNDERSTANDING JAVA

Java, Java, Java. It seems to be everywhere. It's not coffee, although there are coffee-related stories as to how it got its name.

 **Java** A new programming language, like HTML, developed by Sun Microsystems.

Java allows a browser to download small programs (sometimes called Java applets) from a Web server along with a web page, in the same way images are downloaded. These programs then execute on the client PC to add animation or respond to what a user does. It allows interaction between the Web page and the user. Before Java, intranet applications were limited to static displays, occasionally updated from a Web server.

What Java means for intranets is that Web pages are going to become much more interactive as more and more programs incorporate the capabilities of the language. Application software vendors such as Dun & Bradstreet and PeopleSoft have announced products that are Java-enabled. A Dun & Bradstreet application will allow users to download, fill out, and file purchase requisitions for approval. With Java, a full-blown client for every application will not need to be loaded on client PCs. All that will be needed on the client PC is a browser.

**See Java in Action**   If you have access to the Internet, you can see some innovative uses of Java at the archive of Cool Applets at the Sun Java site:

**http://www.javasoft.com/applets/applets.html**

# Understanding VRML

VRML, Virtual Reality Modeling Language, is probably the hottest new technology today, and its potential impact on how the world will conduct business in the near future is extraordinary. As the name implies, it's a language. Images created using VRML are presented on your browser as three dimensional (sort of like getting 3-D glasses to watch a movie!). Further, these images can be rotated and viewed from all sides, and you can zoom in for close-ups or zoom out for wider perspectives.

**VRML**    An acronym for Virtual Reality Modeling Language. It is being pronounced "ver-mul" by some and "ver-mel" by others, so take your pick.

While VRML objects are fun to play with, the technology has many obvious practical applications for business:

- Architects can build a model of a building, and construction engineers or electricians can look at it from different perspectives or move through it room by room.

- Automobile designers, or designers of any type of equipment, can build and work with engineering drawings.

- Instead of sending out hard-to-understand written instructions for assembling a toy or some other consumer product, manufacturers could provide Internet access to VRML-based materials.

- Customer service agents on an intranet could view different models of products while interacting with customers on the phone.

This is a technology where imagination is the limit for applications. If you have Internet access, you can learn more about VRML at **http://www.sdsc.edu/vrml**.

# USING GROUPWARE

In Lesson 1, we touched briefly on the effect of intranet technology on existing software applications and systems. Probably nowhere is the effect more pronounced than on a software type called *groupware*.

Groupware is another term that doesn't have a hard and fast definition and that means different things to different people. Generally speaking, when groupware is mentioned, it refers to a software system or environment on a network that facilitates people collaborating on a work product—document or documents. For corporations, it offers the opportunity for productivity improvements in the way people work together.

Products positioned as Groupware typically include such features as:

- Document management for check-in, check-out, and version control of documents in a database.

- Workflow to control the movement of document images through work processes.

- Full-text searching to find occurrences of words or phrases in all documents in a database.

- Project control and reporting to plan and monitor work efforts.

- Calendar and schedule functions for setting and tracking appointments, meetings, and "to-do" lists.

- E-mail to exchange information with coworkers.

Lotus Notes is probably the best-known groupware product on the market today. But groupware is a very dynamic area of software development, with new products being introduced at a frantic pace. Some products claim to provide comprehensive groupware solutions; others address specific functions. For example, Livelink from Open Text Corporation advertises a complete suite of groupware products while On-Time from Campbell Services, Inc. is testing its calendar and schedule functions for Web use.

The bottom line is that groupware applications are coming to intranets.

So what does it all mean to you as an intranet user? Java, VRML, and groupware activity and product introductions are important indications of an ever-increasing interest in and use of intranet technology for all types of corporate computing. More and more capabilities will be added and assimilated into what you're doing today.

In this lesson, you learned about several key technologies that will affect your intranet use in the future. In the next lesson, you learn about sharing and receiving information outside your intranet and onto the Internet.

# Part 3

## Moving Beyond Corporate Boundaries

# CONNECTING TO THE INTERNET

*In this lesson, you learn the benefits and risks associated with establishing an Internet connection to corporate networks, what's being done to minimize the risks, and how to configure your browser to access the Internet.*

## WHEN AN INTRANET IS NO LONGER JUST "INTRA"...

If you have an intranet, two related questions will arise at some point:

1. Should and how can the information on your intranet be made available to outsiders via the Internet?

2. Should intranet users have access to the resources of the Internet?

 **Red Alert**   Information Systems security is vital to an organization's success. Everyone in a networked environment must be aware of dangers and always vigilant against threats.

## THE BENEFITS OF CONNECTING TO THE INTERNET

There is a big world out there—full of customers, suppliers, and information sources. The Internet is a breakthrough in facilitating communication and commerce among these entities. We are just beginning to get a glimpse of what's possible when corporations adopt the technology. Many benefits accrue from giving employees access to the Internet as well as allowing appropriate Internet users to access selected information in corporate databases.

## LETTING OUTSIDERS ACCESS INFORMATION ON INTRANETS

Many corporations are establishing home pages on the Internet. Initially, most of these pages only provided passive viewing of general information about a corporation, its products, and its services. As technological capabilities increased, corporations began to see ways to increase productivity and save money by allowing outside users to access data from corporate systems through their Internet connection.

Suppliers and customers are very receptive to pursuing the concept. The Internet backbone is much cheaper than leasing a private line for business-to-business usage, and this mode of operation can reduce many other overhead costs. Customers like on-demand access to their records and the ability to check the status of shipments, troubleshoot problems with products, or view catalogs and place orders.

## LETTING INSIDERS ACCESS INFORMATION ON THE INTERNET

There are also many valuable business resources available to intranet users connected to the Internet. Search engines similar to those discussed in Lesson 18 and other tools offer capabilities for doing research on just about any topic. Newspapers and magazines are online; patent information and many other government databases are easily accessible; software from vendors can be downloaded; newsgroups, where discussions take place and ideas are interchanged, exist on over 10,000 topics. The Internet can be your library, expert consultant, and communications system all rolled into one.

What's even better is that everything you have learned about your intranet is applicable to the Internet. Nothing needs to be re-learned. When you click a link to the Internet or type in an Internet address, you're on your way. Note that there are a few additional functions you can do on the Internet that don't have meaning on an intranet (such as accessing Gopher or Veronica servers, shopping…). These topics are covered either in *10 Minute Guide to Netscape for Windows 95* or *10 Minute Guide to Microsoft Internet Explorer*, depending on your browser.

# CONNECTING TO THE INTERNET: THE RISKS

So, why isn't everyone connecting corporate networks to the Internet as fast as possible, to reap these benefits for employees, customers, and suppliers?

There's a simple answer right now. An Internet connection, whether to share or receive information, makes corporate networks more vulnerable to harm. People who want to do mischief, cause damage, or improperly obtain proprietary information are constantly experimenting with ways to do so. Almost every day you read about *hackers* penetrating computer security with some new approach or deciphering the newest data encryption technique.

Frequently, the major consideration by corporations in connecting to the Internet is not justifying the cost/benefit, but rather, assuring management that it is safe to do so.

# USING FIREWALLS FOR PROTECTION

To minimize the risk of unauthorized access to your systems and data, *firewalls* may be used.

 **Firewall**   A hardware and software security system established to prevent unauthorized access to a corporate network (intranet) or the Internet.

Firewall systems are usually either *packet filters* or *proxies*. Packet filters check each packet of information at the network level and don't allow any packets that are determined to be a security risk through.

**Packets**    Small chunks of information.

Typical proxies on an internal network accept a connection from a user, make a decision on whether that user is authorized to use the proxy, and then complete a connection on behalf of the authorized user to an Internet destination. Essentially for World Wide Web access, proxies take the user's requests (URLs), make the Internet connection, receive the information from the Internet, and pass it along to the user.

**Proxy**    Just as in real life, a proxy is an agent, a representative, or a go-between that acts on behalf of another. Network proxies are software that act on behalf of a user to transfer information to and from the Internet through a firewall.

Firewalls are available for free from sites containing public domain software; numerous commercial packages can be purchased at various price and functionality levels.

## How Do Firewalls Work?

As illustrated in Figure 22.1, firewalls are designed to detect and prevent unauthorized connections and access from the outside world.

Firewalls vary widely in philosophy and complexity:

- Some permit all access that is not specifically forbidden.

- Some forbid all access that is not specifically permitted.

- Some permit only e-mail traffic.

- Sophisticated firewalls can block some incoming traffic but permit users on the inside to communicate freely with the outside.

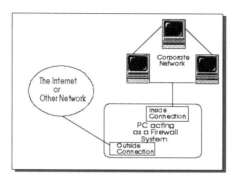

**FIGURE 22.1**    A firewall.

 **Immune System?**    Firewalls do not work particularly well against viruses. It is better to have network level and PC level protection for viruses than it is to try to detect and intercept them only on a firewall.

# HOW DO YOU RECOGNIZE THE PRESENCE OF A FIREWALL?

There are two basic reasons why you might not be able to access the Internet from your intranet. The first reason is that your intranet may not be connected to the Internet. There's not much you can do about this. The other is that you may encounter a firewall. When you encounter a firewall, you will be asked for some sort of identifying information, such as a password; or you will have to configure your browser's proxies for access. In any case, you will be able to access information through the firewall only if you can identify yourself as having the necessary clearance.

# CONFIGURING PROXIES

As mentioned previously, a network *proxy* is the go-between for your computer and the Internet. A network proxy is used to access the Internet through a firewall. If you have a direct connection to the Internet, you do not need to configure proxies. If you have a firewall, you will need to configure proxies to access the Internet.

**Ask and You Shall Receive**  Configuring proxies requires input from your system administrator. First, determine from the administrator if you are to do a manual or automatic configuration, then write down the information provided, and follow the automatic or manual configuration steps below as appropriate for your browser.

## AUTOMATIC PROXY CONFIGURATION FOR NETSCAPE

In some cases the system administrator will have set up a proxy configuration file for Netscape to use. If this is the case, ask your system administrator for the location (URL) of the file and follow the steps below.

1. Open the Options menu and click Network Preferences. The Preferences dialog box is displayed.

2. Click the Proxy tab. From the Proxy window click the button beside the **Automatic Proxy Configuration** (see Figure 22.2).

3. Enter the URL provided by your system administrator in the box beside Configuration Location.

4. Click OK to return to the current Web page.

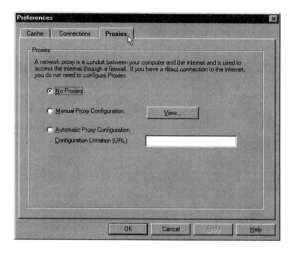

The Proxies tab.

## MANUAL PROXY CONFIGURATION FOR NETSCAPE

If your system administrator has not set up automatic proxy configuration, ask for the manual proxy configuration information and follow the steps below.

1. Open the Options menu and click Network Preferences. The Preferences dialog box is displayed.

2. Click the Proxies tab at the top of the window to bring it to the front, as shown in Figure 22.2.

3. To manually configure your proxies, click the option button beside **Manual Proxy Configuration** and then click the View button. The Proxies dialog box appears, as shown in Figure 22.3

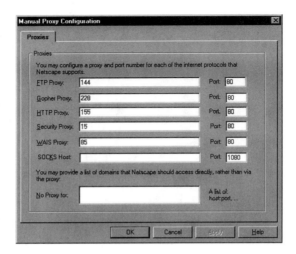

**FIGURE 22.3**    Proxies and ports.

**4.** Enter the Proxies and Ports values as directed by your system administrator. Note that you will need a proxy and port for each Internet capability (protocol) you plan on using.

**5.** Click OK.

**6.** Click OK on the Preferences Dialog window and you are returned to the page you were viewing.

## AUTOMATIC PROXY CONFIGURATION FOR INTERNET EXPLORER

Since you cannot configure proxies for Internet Explorer, the system administrator will have set up a proxy configuration file. Windows 95 can be configured to find this file that contains the information to access the Internet through your firewall. Ask your system administrator for the location and port of the proxy and follow the steps below.

**1.** You will access the control panel through the Start Menu's Settings option (see Figure 22.4).

**2.** Double-click the Internet icon, and the Internet Properties dialog box appears, as shown in Figure 22.5.

FIGURE 22.4    Internet icon.

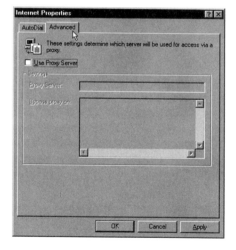

FIGURE 22.5    Internet Properties Window.

**3.** Click the Advanced tab.

4. Click the check box to the left of Use Proxy Server in the settings area (see Figure 22.6). Type the location and the port next to Proxy Server.

5. If you need to keep the Internet Properties window open, click Apply. Otherwise, click OK to save the settings and close the Internet Properties window.

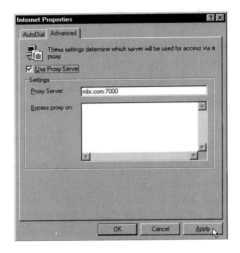

**Figure 22.6**    Completing Automatic Proxy configuration.

6. Close (X) the Control Panel window and re-access your intranet.

7. Now when you try to access the Internet, Windows 95 takes you to your selected proxy server, which takes you through the firewall and onto the Internet.

## Helpful Internet Sites

By now you may have some detailed questions about sharing and protecting the systems and data that make up your intranet. If you have access to the Internet and want to learn more about external access and security considerations, you can get more information from sites listed in Table 22.1.

**TABLE 22.1    SECURITY SOURCES**

| SITE | INFORMATION |
| --- | --- |
| **http://www.ncsa.com** | Get a free guide and catalog at the National Computer Security Association site. |
| **http://www.iss.net/ sec_info/faq.html** | Access files with Frequently Asked Questions (FAQ) at the Internet Security Systems, Inc. site. |
| **http://www.iss.net/ sec_info/maillis.html** | Subscribe to security-related mailing lists at the Internet Security Systems, Inc. site. |

In this lesson, you learned about connecting corporate networks to the Internet.

Congratulations! You are well on your way to surfing your company's intranet like a pro. Whether you already access an intranet or will access one shortly, you have at your disposal the tools for success. Just keep Que's *10 Minute Guide to the Intranet* within reach. Then, whenever you hit a snag or forget a command, flip to the corresponding lesson for quick and easy assistance.

# WINDOWS 95 PRIMER

*Microsoft Windows 95 is a graphical operating system that makes your computer easy to use by providing menus and pictures from which you select. Before you can take advantage of it, however, you must learn some Windows 95 basics.*

## A FIRST LOOK AT WINDOWS 95

You don't really have to start Windows 95 because it starts automatically when you turn on your PC. After the initial startup screens, you arrive at a screen something like the one shown in Figure A.1.

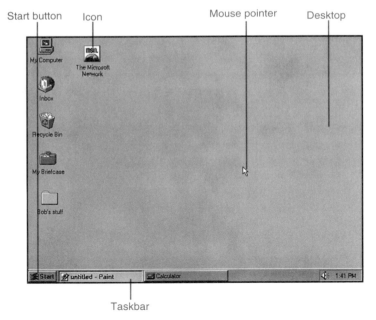

**FIGURE A.1** The Windows 95 screen.

## PARTS OF THE SCREEN

As you can see in Figure A.1, the Windows 95 screen contains many special elements and controls. Here's a brief summary:

- The background on which all the pictures and boxes rest is the *desktop*.

- The *taskbar* shows a button for each window and program that is open. You can switch between open windows and programs by clicking the taskbar button for the one you want. (Notice how the open programs look on the taskbar in Figure A.1.)

- The *Start button* opens a menu system from which you can start programs. To use it, you click the Start button, and then you click a selection in each successive menu that appears.

- The *icons* that appear on your desktop give you access to certain programs and computer components. You activate an icon by double-clicking it.

- The *mouse pointer* moves around the screen in relation to your movement of the mouse. You use the mouse pointer to indicate what you want to select or work with.

You'll learn more about these elements as you work through the rest of the appendix.

**Also Appearing...**   If your computer has Microsoft Office installed on it, the Office Shortcuts toolbar also appears on-screen. It's a series of little pictures (strung together horizontally) that represent Office programs. Hold the mouse over a picture (icon) to see what it does; click it to launch the program. See your Microsoft Office documentation to learn more.

## Using a Mouse

To work most efficiently in Windows, you need a mouse. You will perform the following mouse actions as you work:

- **Point**   To move the mouse so that the mouse pointer is on the specified item. The tip of the mouse pointer must touch the item.

- **Click**   To move the pointer onto the specified item and press and release the left mouse button once. Unless you're told to do otherwise (i.e., to right-click), you always use the left mouse button. Clicking usually selects an item.

- **Double-click**   To move the pointer onto the specified item and press and release the left mouse button twice quickly. Double-clicking usually activates an item.

- **Drag**   To move the mouse pointer onto the specified item, press and hold down the left mouse button, and move the mouse to a new location. Unless you're told to do otherwise (i.e., to right-drag), you drag with the left mouse button.

## Controlling a Window with the Mouse

Windows are the heart of the Windows 95 program. Windows 95 sections off rectangular areas called "windows" for particular purposes, such as running a program. You control a window using the techniques described in Figure A.2.

**Scroll Bars**   If your window contains more icons than it can display at once, scroll bars appear on the bottom and/or right edges of the window. To move through the window's contents, click an arrow button at either end of a scroll bar to move in that direction, or drag the gray bar in the direction you want to move.

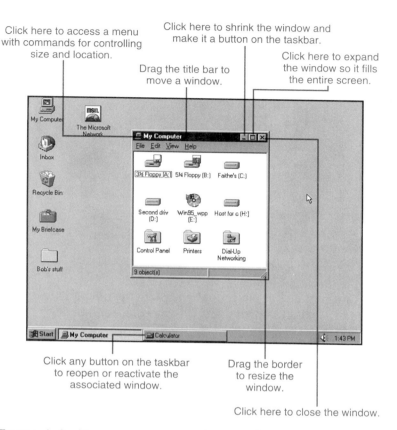

Click here to access a menu with commands for controlling size and location.

Click here to shrink the window and make it a button on the taskbar.

Drag the title bar to move a window.

Click here to expand the window so it fills the entire screen.

Click any button on the taskbar to reopen or reactivate the associated window.

Drag the border to resize the window.

Click here to close the window.

**FIGURE A.2**     You use your mouse to control windows.

# GETTING HELP

Windows 95 comes with a great online Help system. To access it, click the Start button and click Help. You see the box shown in Figure A.3.

This box contains three tabs (Contents, Index, and Find), each of which provides you with a different type of help. The Contents tab appears on top first. To move to a tab, click it. Here's how to use each tab:

FIGURE A.3    Windows offers several kinds of help.

- **Contents**   Double-click any book to open it and see its sub-books and documents. Double-click a sub-book or document to open it.

- **Index**   Type the word you want to look up, and the Index list scrolls to that part of the alphabetical listing. When you see the topic that you want to read in the list, double-click it.

- **Find**   The first time you click this tab, Windows tells you it needs to create a list. Click Next and then Finish to allow this. When Windows finishes, you see the main Find tab. Type the word you want to find in the top text box. Then click a word in the middle box to narrow the search. Finally, review the list of Help topics at the bottom, and double-click the one you want to read.

When you finish reading about a document, click Help Topics to return to the main Help screen, or click Back to return to the previous Help topic. When you finish with the Help system itself, click the window's Close (X) button to exit.

# STARTING A PROGRAM

Of the many possible ways to start a program, this is the simplest (see Figure A.4):

1. Click the Start button.

2. Click Programs.

3. Click the group that contains the program you want to start (such as **Microsoft Office 95**).

4. Click the program you want to start (such as **Microsoft Access**).

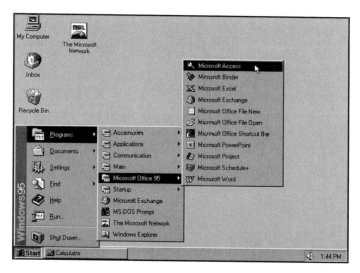

**FIGURE A. 4**   Work through the Start menu and its successive submenus until you find the program you want to start.

Another way to start a program is to open a document that you created in that program. The program automatically opens when the document opens. For example, double-click a document file in My Computer or Windows Explorer, or click the **Start** button and select a recently used document from the **Documents** menu. Windows immediately starts the program in which you created the file and opens the file.

You can also start a program by double-clicking its shortcut icon on the desktop. Shortcut icons are links to other files. When you use a shortcut, Windows simply follows the link back to the original file. If you find that you use any document or program frequently, you might consider creating a desktop shortcut for it. To do so, just use the right mouse button to drag an object out of Windows Explorer or My Computer and onto the desktop. In the shortcut menu that appears, select Create Shortcut(s) Here.

## USING MENUS

Almost every Windows program has a menu bar that contains menus. The menu names appear across the top of the screen in a row. To open a menu, click its name. The menu drops down, displaying its commands (see Figure A.5). To select a command, you click it.

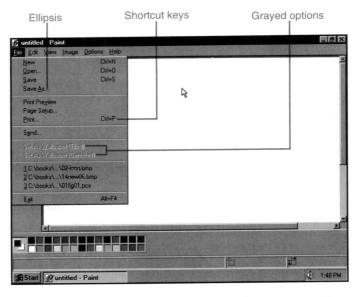

**FIGURE A.5**   A menu lists various commands you can perform.

Usually, when you select a command, Windows 95 executes the command immediately. However, the following exceptions break that rule:

- If the command name is gray (instead of black), the command is unavailable at the moment and you cannot choose it.

- If the command name is followed by an arrow (as the selections on the Start menu are), selecting the command causes another menu to appear, from which you must make another selection.

- If the command is followed by an ellipsis (three dots), selecting it will cause a dialog box to appear. You'll learn about dialog boxes later in this appendix.

 **Shortcut Keys**  Key names appear after some command names (for example, Enter appears to the right of the Open command, and F8 appears next to the Copy command). These are shortcut keys. You use these keys to perform the command without opening the menu.

## USING SHORTCUT MENUS

A new feature in Windows 95 is the shortcut menu. Right-click any object (icon, screen element, file, or folder, for example), and a shortcut menu like the one shown in Figure A.6 appears. The shortcut menu contains commands that apply only to the selected object. Click any command to select it, or click outside the menu to cancel.

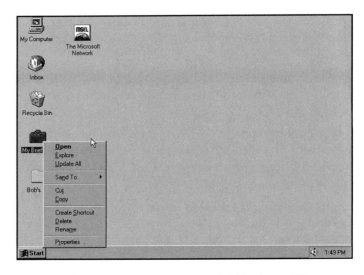

**FIGURE A.6**    Shortcut menus are new in Windows 95.

# NAVIGATING DIALOG BOXES

A *dialog box* is the operating system's way of requesting additional information or giving you information. For example, if you choose Print from the File menu of the WordPad application, you see a dialog box something like the one shown in Figure A.7. (The options it displays will vary from system to system.)

> **Dialog Box**    A type of box that a program displays when it needs more information from you or when it needs to give you information. It's the closest thing to a "dialog" that you can have with your program.

Each dialog box contains one or more of the following elements:

- *Tabs* bring up additional "pages" of options you can choose. Click a tab to activate it.

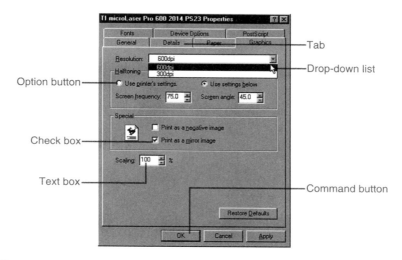

**FIGURE A.7**    A dialog box often requests additional information.

- *List boxes* display available choices. Click any item on the list to select it. If the entire list is not visible, use the scroll bar to find additional choices.

- *Drop-down lists* are similar to list boxes, but only one item in the list is shown. To see the rest of the list, click the drop-down arrow (to the right of the list box). Then click an item to select it.

- *Text boxes* enable you to type in an entry. Just click inside the text box and type. Text boxes that expect numeric input usually have up and down arrow buttons (increment buttons) that let you bump the number up and down.

- *Check boxes* enable you to turn individual options on or off. Click a check box to turn it on or off. Each check box is an independent unit that doesn't affect other check boxes.

- *Option buttons* are like check boxes, except that option buttons appear in groups and you can select only one.

When you select an option button, the program automatically deselects whichever one was previously selected. Click a button to activate it.

* *Command buttons* perform an action, such as executing the options you set, closing the dialog box, or opening another dialog box. To select a command button, click it.

# FROM HERE...

If you need more help with Windows 95, I suggest that you pick up one of these books:

*The Complete Idiot's Guide to Windows 95* by Paul McFedries

*Windows 95 Cheat Sheet* by Joe Kraynak

*The Big Basics Book of Windows 95* by Shelley O'Hara, Jennifer Fulton, and Ed Guilford

# INDEX

# P-Q

# Check out Que® Books on the World Wide Web
## http://www.mcp.com/que

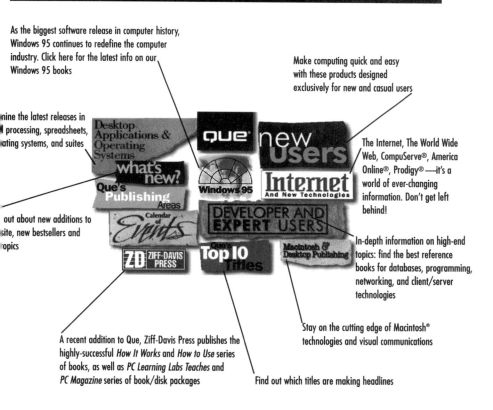

As the biggest software release in computer history, Windows 95 continues to redefine the computer industry. Click here for the latest info on our Windows 95 books

Make computing quick and easy with these products designed exclusively for new and casual users

nine the latest releases in processing, spreadsheets, ating systems, and suites

The Internet, The World Wide Web, CompuServe®, America Online®, Prodigy® —it's a world of ever-changing information. Don't get left behind!

out about new additions to site, new bestsellers and opics

In-depth information on high-end topics: find the best reference books for databases, programming, networking, and client/server technologies

A recent addition to Que, Ziff-Davis Press publishes the highly-successful *How It Works* and *How to Use* series of books, as well as *PC Learning Labs Teaches* and *PC Magazine* series of book/disk packages

Stay on the cutting edge of Macintosh® technologies and visual communications

Find out which titles are making headlines

6 separate publishing groups, Que develops products for many specific market segments and areas of mputer technology. Explore our Web Site and you'll find information on best-selling titles, newly published titles, upcoming products, authors, and much more.

- Stay informed on the latest industry trends and products available
- Visit our online bookstore for the latest information and editions
- Download software from Que's library of the best shareware and freeware

# Complete and Return this Card
# for a *FREE* Computer Book Catalog

Thank you for purchasing this book! You have purchased a superior computer book written expressly for your needs. To continue to provide the kind of up-to-date, pertinent coverage you've come to expect from us, we need to hear from you. Please take a minute to complete and return this self-addressed, postage-paid form. In return, we'll send you a free catalog of all our computer books on topics ranging from word processing to programming and the internet.

Mr. ☐   Mrs. ☐   Ms. ☐   Dr. ☐

Name (first) ☐☐☐☐☐☐☐☐   (M.I.) ☐   (last) ☐☐☐☐☐☐☐☐☐☐☐

Address ☐☐☐☐☐☐☐☐☐☐☐☐☐☐☐☐☐☐☐☐☐

☐☐☐☐☐☐☐☐☐☐☐☐☐☐☐☐☐☐☐☐☐

City ☐☐☐☐☐☐☐☐☐☐☐   State ☐☐   Zip ☐☐☐☐☐ ☐☐☐☐

Phone ☐☐☐ ☐☐☐ ☐☐☐☐   Fax ☐☐☐ ☐☐☐ ☐☐☐☐

Company Name ☐☐☐☐☐☐☐☐☐☐☐☐☐☐☐☐☐☐

E-mail address ☐☐☐☐☐☐☐☐☐☐☐☐☐☐☐☐☐☐☐☐☐☐☐

## 1. Please check at least (3) influencing factors for purchasing this book.

Front or back cover information on book ......... ☐
Special approach to the content ...................... ☐
Completeness of content .............................. ☐
Author's reputation ..................................... ☐
Publisher's reputation .................................. ☐
Book cover design or layout .......................... ☐
Index or table of contents of book .................. ☐
Price of book ............................................. ☐
Special effects, graphics, illustrations .............. ☐
Other (Please specify): _____ ☐

## 2. How did you first learn about this book?

Internet Site ............................................... ☐
Saw in Macmillan Computer
    Publishing catalog .................................. ☐
Recommended by store personnel .................... ☐
Saw the book on bookshelf at store .................. ☐
Recommended by a friend .............................. ☐
Received advertisement in the mail .................. ☐
Saw an advertisement in: _____ ☐
Read book review in: _____ ☐
Other (Please specify): _____ ☐

## 3. How many computer books have you purchased in the last six months?

This book only .......... ☐   3 to 5 books ........ ☐
2 books .................... ☐   More than 5 ........ ☐

## 4. Where did you purchase this book?

Bookstore ................................................... ☐
Computer Store ........................................... ☐
Consumer Electronics Store ............................ ☐
Department Store ......................................... ☐
Office Club ................................................. ☐
Warehouse Club ........................................... ☐
Mail Order ................................................. ☐
Direct from Publisher .................................... ☐
Internet site ............................................... ☐
Other (Please specify): ................................. ☐

## 5. How long have you been using a computer?

Less than 6 months .. ☐   6 months to a year ..... ☐
1 to 3 years .............. ☐   More than 3 years ...... ☐

## 6. What is your level of experience with personal computers and with the subject of this book?

|  | With PC's | With subject of book |
|---|---|---|
| New | ☐ | ☐ |
| Casual | ☐ | ☐ |
| Accomplished | ☐ | ☐ |
| Expert | ☐ | ☐ |

**Source Code** — ISBN: 0-7897-0855-8

## 7. Which of the following best describes your job title?

Administrative Assistant ........................... ☐
Coordinator ............................................... ☐
Manager/Supervisor .................................. ☐
Director ..................................................... ☐
Vice President ........................................... ☐
President/CEO/COO .................................. ☐
Lawyer/Doctor/Medical Professional .......... ☐
Teacher/Educator/Trainer ......................... ☐
Engineer/Technician ................................. ☐
Consultant ................................................. ☐
Not employed/Student/Retired .................... ☐
Other (Please specify): ............................. ☐

## 8. Which of the following best describes the area of the company your job title falls under?

Accounting ................................................ ☐
Engineering ............................................... ☐
Manufacturing ........................................... ☐
Marketing .................................................. ☐
Operations ................................................. ☐
Sales .......................................................... ☐
Other (Please specify): ............................. ☐

## 9. What is your age?

Under 20 ................................................... ☐
21-29 ......................................................... ☐
30-39 ......................................................... ☐
40-49 ......................................................... ☐
50-59 ......................................................... ☐
60-over ...................................................... ☐

## 10. Are you:

Male ........................................................... ☐
Female ....................................................... ☐

## 11. Which computer publications do you read regularly? (Please list)

_____
_____
_____
_____
_____
_____
_____
_____
_____
_____

*Comments*: _____
_____
_____

Fold here and scotch-tape to m

⑀⑂⑀⑂⑀⑂⑀⑂⑀⑂⑀⑂⑀⑂⑀